KITCHEN LIBRARY
Desserts

KITCHEN LIBRARY
Desserts

MURDOCH BOOKS

contents

A SWEET ENDING   7

COLD DESSERTS   8

HOT DESSERTS   90

PIES, TARTS AND PASTRIES   162

SMALL BITES   242

INDEX   298

A Sweet Ending

It's a rare person who doesn't like dessert. Whether light and refreshingly fruity or luxuriant with chocolate, nuts or mascarpone cheese, a sweet ending is arguably the most anticipated part of any meal. In these days of busy lives with little time for regular dessert making, a homemade dessert truly is a treat; host a dinner party and finish with some delectable dessert and your guests will feel honoured indeed. And nothing spreads love and goodwill around the weekday family dinner table like the occasional homey dessert, whether pumpkin pie, cherry pie, rhubarb crumble or a creamy rice pudding.

In *Kitchen Library Desserts*, some familiar favourites that 'mum used to make' have been given a contemporary twist, without straying too far from the spirit of the beloved original. Thus trifle is flavoured with chocolate and cherry, lemon syllabub is perked up with passionfruit and gooey, gorgeous chocolate self-saucing pudding is scented with cinnamon.

When deciding on which dessert to make, consider the dish that comes before it so you can balance your menu accordingly. If it's a hearty meal you'll be serving, such as a roast or a meaty braise, opt for a fruit-based dessert, a sorbet, a mousse or something similarly light. Classics like pears poached in wine, strawberries Romanoff or chocolate bavarois are always popular choices and are quite simple to prepare. Cold weather, or a less substantial main course, allow for something a little more indulgent such as bubbling plum cobbler slathered in whipped cream, a chocolaty cheesecake or a velvety lemon delicious. Whichever scrumptious recipe you choose, you're sure to win favour around the dinner table; after all, no-one refuses a good, homemade dessert.

cold desserts

Pavlova Roll with Raspberry Coulis

🔺 SERVES 8–10

🔺 PREPARATION TIME: 25 MINUTES +

🔺 COOKING TIME: 15 MINUTES

4 egg whites

230 g (8½ oz/1 cup) caster (superfine)
  sugar

1 teaspoon cornflour (cornstarch)

2 teaspoons lemon juice or white vinegar

55 g (2 oz/¼ cup) chopped fresh berries

170 ml (5½ fl oz/⅔ cup) whipping
  cream, whipped

RASPBERRY COULIS

2 tablespoons brandy

250 g (9 oz/2 cups) fresh raspberries

1 tablespoon icing (confectioners') sugar

Brush a 25 x 30 cm (10 x 12 inch) Swiss roll (jelly roll) tin with oil and line with baking paper extending up two sides. Preheat the oven to 180°C (350°F/Gas 4). Beat the egg whites into soft peaks, then gradually add three-quarters of the sugar and beat until thick and glossy. Combine 1 tablespoon of the remaining sugar with the cornflour. Fold into the meringue with the lemon juice or vinegar. Spoon into the tin and smooth. Bake for 12–15 minutes, or until springy.

Put a large sheet of baking paper on top of a tea towel (dish towel) and generously sprinkle with the rest of the sugar. Turn the pavlova onto the baking paper, peel off the lining paper and leave for 3 minutes. Roll up the pavlova from the long side using the tea towel to assist, then cool.

Fold the berries into the whipped cream. Unroll the pavlova, fill with the cream mixture and re-roll without the tea towel and baking paper. Transfer to a plate and refrigerate.

To make the raspberry coulis, put the brandy, raspberries and icing sugar in a food processor and process until well blended. Serve the pavlova roll in slices with the raspberry coulis.

NOTE: If you prefer, a thick fruit purée may be used to fill the roll.

Crema Catalana

1 litre (35 fl oz/4 cups) milk
1 vanilla bean
1 cinnamon stick
zest of 1 small lemon, sliced into strips
2 strips orange zest (2 x 4 cm/
    $^3/_4$ x $1^1/_2$ inches)
8 egg yolks
115 g (4 oz/$^1/_2$ cup) caster (superfine)
    sugar
40 g ($1^1/_2$ oz/$^1/_3$ cup) cornflour
    (cornstarch)
45 g ($1^3/_4$ oz/$^1/_4$ cup) soft brown sugar

Put the milk in a saucepan. Split the vanilla bean lengthways, scrape the seeds into the milk and put the bean in too. Add the cinnamon stick and lemon and orange zest and bring to the boil. Simmer for 5 minutes, then strain and set aside.

Whisk the egg yolks with the caster sugar in a bowl for about 5 minutes, or until pale and creamy. Add the cornflour and mix well. Slowly add the warm milk mixture to the egg and whisk continuously. Return to the pan and cook over medium–low heat, stirring constantly, for 5–10 minutes, or until the mixture is thick and creamy. Do not boil, as it will curdle. Pour into six 250 ml (9 fl oz/1 cup) ramekins or dariole moulds and refrigerate for 6 hours, or overnight.

When ready to serve, sprinkle the custards evenly with brown sugar and grill (broil) for 3 minutes, or until the sugar caramelises.

Devil's Food Cake

🔺 SERVES 8–10
🔺 PREPARATION TIME: 30 MINUTES
🔺 COOKING TIME: 45 MINUTES

280 g (10 oz/1½ cups) soft brown sugar
40 g (1½ oz/⅓ cup) unsweetened cocoa
    powder
250 ml (9 fl oz/1 cup) milk
90 g (3¼ oz) dark chocolate, chopped
125 g (4½ oz) unsalted butter, softened
1 teaspoon natural vanilla extract
2 eggs, separated
185 g (6½ oz/1½ cups) plain
    (all-purpose) flour
1 teaspoon bicarbonate of soda (baking
    soda)
unsweetened cocoa powder, to dust

CHOCOLATE ICING (FROSTING)
50 g (1¾ oz) dark chocolate, chopped
30 g (1 oz) unsalted butter
1 tablespoon icing (confectioners') sugar

FILLING
250 ml (9 fl oz/1 cup) whipping cream
1 tablespoon icing (confectioners') sugar
1 teaspoon natural vanilla extract

Preheat the oven to 160°C (315°F/Gas 2–3). Lightly grease two deep 20 cm (8 inch) round cake tins and line the bases with baking paper. Combine a third of the brown sugar with the cocoa and milk in a small saucepan. Stir over low heat until the sugar and cocoa have dissolved. Remove from the heat and stir in the chocolate, stirring until melted. Cool.

Cream the remaining brown sugar with the butter in a small bowl with electric beaters until light and fluffy. Beat in the vanilla and egg yolks and the cooled chocolate mixture. Transfer to a large bowl and stir in the sifted flour and bicarbonate of soda.

Beat the egg whites in a clean, dry small bowl until soft peaks form. Fold into the chocolate mixture. Divide the mixture evenly between the tins. Bake for 35 minutes, or until a skewer inserted in the centre of the cakes comes out clean. Leave in the tins for 5 minutes before turning out onto a wire rack to cool.

To make the chocolate icing, put the chocolate and butter in a heatproof bowl. Place the bowl over a saucepan of simmering water, making sure it doesn't touch the water, and stir until the mixture is melted and smooth. Gradually add the sifted icing sugar and stir until smooth.

To make the filling, whip the cream, icing sugar and vanilla in a small bowl with electric beaters until stiff peaks form. Spread over one of the cold cakes, top with the second cake and spread with icing, over the top or top and sides. Dust with cocoa powder.

Thai Sticky Rice with Mangoes

🔺 SERVES 4
🔺 PREPARATION TIME: 10 MINUTES +
🔺 COOKING TIME: 1 HOUR 5 MINUTES

400 g (14 oz/2 cups) long-grain
    white rice
1 tablespoon white sesame seeds
250 ml (9 fl oz/1 cup) coconut milk
70 g (2½ oz/½ cup) grated palm sugar
    (jaggery)
2–3 mangoes, peeled, seeded and sliced
60 ml (2 fl oz/¼ cup) coconut cream
mint sprigs, to garnish

Put the rice in a sieve and wash under cold running water until the water runs clear. Put the rice in a glass or ceramic bowl, cover with water and soak overnight, or for at least 12 hours. Drain the rice.

Line a metal or bamboo steamer with a piece of muslin (cheesecloth). Put the rice on top of the muslin and cover the steamer with a tight-fitting lid. Put the steamer over a saucepan or wok of boiling water and steam over medium–low heat for 50 minutes, or until the rice is cooked. Replenish the pot with boiling water as necessary. Transfer the rice to a large bowl and fluff it up with a fork.

Toast the sesame seeds in a frying pan over medium heat for 3–4 minutes, shaking the pan gently until the seeds are golden brown. Remove from the pan immediately to prevent them burning.

Put the coconut milk into a small saucepan, then add the sugar and ¼ teaspoon salt. Slowly bring the mixture to the boil, stirring constantly until the sugar has dissolved. Reduce the heat and simmer for 5 minutes, or until the mixture has slightly thickened. Stir the mixture often while it is simmering, to prevent it sticking to the bottom of the pan.

Slowly pour the coconut milk over the top of the rice. Use a fork to lift and fluff up the rice. Do not stir the liquid through, otherwise the rice will become too gluggy. Let the rice mixture rest for 20 minutes before carefully spooning it into the centre of four warmed serving bowls. Arrange the mango slices on the rice mounds. Spoon some coconut cream over the rice, sprinkle over the sesame seeds and garnish with the mint.

Rice Ice Cream

⚶ SERVES 4
⚶ PREPARATION TIME: 20 MINUTES +
⚶ COOKING TIME: 25 MINUTES

110 g (3¾ oz/½ cup) risotto rice
750 ml (26 fl oz/3 cups) milk
1 vanilla bean
55 g (2¼ oz/¼ cup) sugar
500 ml (17 fl oz/2 cups) thick
    (double/heavy) cream
3 teaspoons icing (confectioners') sugar
2 tablespoons finely chopped
    candied citron

CUSTARD
125 ml (4 fl oz/½ cup) milk
3 egg yolks
110 g (3¾ oz/½ cup) sugar

Put the rice in a saucepan, add the milk, vanilla bean, sugar and a pinch of salt. Bring to the boil over medium heat, stirring constantly. Reduce the heat to low and simmer for about 12 minutes. Remove the rice from the heat and set aside for about 2 hours to cool completely.

Pour the contents of the pan through a colander and drain away the excess liquid. Allow the rice stand for 30 minutes.

To make the custard, heat the milk in a saucepan over medium heat until it is almost boiling. In a bowl, whisk together the egg yolks and sugar, and add the milk. Mix well. Rinse the pan and return the milk mixture to the pan. Cook, stirring constantly, over a low heat until the custard thickens and will easily coat the back of a wooden spoon. Remove the custard from the heat and allow to cool.

Transfer the rice to a bowl, remove the vanilla bean, add the custard and mix well. Add the cream, icing sugar and candied citron, and stir well to combine.

Pour the mixture into a shallow metal tray and freeze for 1 hour. Take the tray out of the freezer and give the mixture a good stir, then refreeze. Repeat this process four times until the mixture is almost solid. The more you stir, the less icy the mixture. Alternatively, you can freeze the mixture in an ice-cream machine, following the manufacturer's instructions.

Remove the ice cream from the freezer 10 minutes before serving to soften. If it is too frozen the rice grains will be very hard.

Pears Poached in Wine

🌿 SERVES 4

🌿 PREPARATION TIME: 20 MINUTES +

🌿 COOKING TIME: 45 MINUTES

4 firm pears
750 ml (26 fl oz/3 cups) good-quality
    red wine
175 g (6 oz/³/4 cup) caster (superfine)
    sugar
1 cinnamon stick
60 ml (2 fl oz/¹/4 cup) orange juice
5 cm (2 inch) piece orange peel
200 g (7 oz) mascarpone cheese, to serve

Peel the pears, being careful to keep the pears whole with the stalks still attached.

Put the wine, sugar, cinnamon stick, orange juice and peel in a saucepan that is large enough for the pears to stand upright. Stir over medium heat until the sugar is dissolved. Add the pears to the saucepan and stir gently to coat. The pears should be almost covered with the wine mixture. Cover the pan and simmer for 20–25 minutes, or until the pears are cooked. Allow to cool in the syrup.

Remove the pears with a slotted spoon. Bring the liquid to the boil and boil rapidly until about 185 ml (6 fl oz/³/4 cup) of liquid remains. Serve the pears with a little syrup and some mascarpone.

Sago Pudding

🌿 SERVES 6

🌿 PREPARATION TIME: 20 MINUTES +

🌿 TOTAL COOKING TIME: 20 MINUTES

200 g (7 oz/1 cup) sago
185 g (6¹/2 oz/1 cup) lightly packed soft
    brown sugar
250 ml (9 fl oz/1 cup) coconut cream,
    well chilled

Soak the sago in 750 ml (26 fl oz/3 cups) water for 1 hour. Pour into a saucepan, add 2 tablespoons of the sugar and bring to the boil over low heat, stirring constantly. Reduce the heat and simmer, stirring occasionally, for 8 minutes. Cover and cook for 2–3 minutes, or until the mixture becomes thick and the sago grains are translucent.

Half fill six wet 125 ml (4 fl oz/¹/2 cup) moulds with the sago mixture. Refrigerate for 2 hours, or until set.

Combine the remaining sugar with 250 ml (9 fl oz/ 1 cup) water in a small saucepan and cook over low heat until the sugar dissolves. Simmer for 5–7 minutes, or until the syrup thickens. Remove from the heat and cool.

To serve, unmould the sago by wiping a cloth dipped in hot water over the mould and turn out onto the plate. Top with the sugar syrup and coconut cream.

Pears Poached in Wine

Chocolate Cherry Trifle

🔥 SERVES 6
🔥 PREPARATION TIME: 30 MINUTES +
🔥 COOKING TIME: 10 MINUTES

350 g (12 oz) ready-made chocolate cake
900 g (2 lb) tinned pitted dark cherries
60 ml (2 fl oz/¼ cup) Kirsch or cherry
   liqueur
30 g (1 oz/¼ cup) slivered almonds,
   toasted
whipped cream, extra, to serve

CUSTARD
185 ml (6 fl oz/¾ cup) whipping cream
2 egg yolks
2 tablespoons sugar
1 tablespoon cornflour (cornstarch)
250 ml (9 fl oz/1 cup) milk
1 teaspoon natural vanilla extract

Cut the cake into thin strips. Line the base of a 1.75 litre (61 fl oz/7 cup) serving bowl with one-third of the cake.

Drain the cherries, reserving the juice. Combine 250 ml (9 fl oz/1 cup) of the juice with the liqueur and sprinkle some liberally over the cake. Spoon some cherries over the cake.

To make the custard, lightly whip the cream and set it aside. Whisk the egg yolks, sugar and cornflour in a heatproof bowl until thick and pale. Heat the milk in a saucepan until almost boiling. Remove from the heat and add gradually to the egg mixture, beating constantly. Return to a clean saucepan and stir over medium heat for 5 minutes, or until the custard boils and thickens. Remove from the heat and add the vanilla. Cover the surface with plastic wrap and allow to cool, then fold in the whipped cream.

To assemble, spoon a third of the custard over the cherries and cake in the bowl. Top with more cake, syrup, cherries and custard. Repeat the layering process, ending with custard on top. Cover and refrigerate for 3–4 hours. Decorate with almonds and whipped cream.

Praline Ice Cream with Caramel Bark

🔺 SERVES 4

🔺 PREPARATION TIME: 25 MINUTES +

🔺 COOKING TIME: 10 MINUTES

70 g (2½ oz) blanched almonds, toasted
55 g (2 oz/¼ cup) caster (superfine)
   sugar
125 g (4½ oz) white chocolate, chopped
185 ml (6 fl oz/¾ cup) whipping cream
250 g (9 oz) mascarpone cheese
2 tablespoons sugar

To make the praline, line a baking tray with foil, brush the foil lightly with oil and put the almonds on the foil.

Put the caster sugar in a small saucepan over low heat. Tilt the saucepan slightly, but do not stir, and watch until the sugar melts and turns golden – this should take 3–5 minutes. Pour the caramel over the almonds and leave until set and cold. Break into chunks, put in a plastic bag and crush with a rolling pin, or process briefly in a food processor until crumbly.

Put the white chocolate in a heatproof bowl. Half-fill a saucepan with water and bring to the boil, then remove the pan from the heat. Sit the bowl over the pan, making sure the base of the bowl doesn't touch the water. Stir occasionally until the chocolate has melted. Set aside to cool.

Whip the cream until stiff peaks form. Put the mascarpone and melted chocolate in a large bowl and stir to combine. Using a metal spoon, fold in the cream and crushed praline. Transfer to a 1 litre (35 fl oz/ 4 cup) metal tin, cover the surface with baking paper and freeze for 6 hours, or overnight. Remove from the freezer 15 minutes before serving, to soften slightly.

To make the caramel bark, line a baking tray with foil and brush lightly with oil. Sprinkle the sugar evenly onto the tray and place under a hot grill (broiler) for 2 minutes, until the sugar has melted and is golden. Check frequently towards the end of cooking time, as the sugar may burn quickly. Remove from the heat, leave until set and completely cold, then break into shards. Serve with the ice cream.

Strawberries Romanoff

⚘ SERVES 4
⚘ PREPARATION TIME: 20 MINUTES +
⚘ COOKING TIME: NIL

750 g (1 lb 10 oz) strawberries, quartered
2 tablespoons Cointreau
1/4 teaspoon finely grated orange zest
1 tablespoon caster (superfine) sugar
125 ml (4 fl oz/1/2 cup) whipping cream
2 tablespoons icing (confectioners') sugar

Combine the strawberries, Cointreau, orange zest and caster sugar in a large bowl, cover and refrigerate for 1 hour. Drain the strawberries, reserving any juices. Purée about one-quarter of the berries with the reserved juices.

Divide the remaining berries among four glasses. Beat the cream and icing sugar until soft peaks form, then fold the berry purée through the whipped cream. Spoon the mixture over the top of the strawberries, cover and refrigerate until required.

Fruit Kebabs with Honey Cardamom Syrup

⚘ MAKES 8
⚘ PREPARATION TIME: 20 MINUTES +
⚘ COOKING TIME: 5 MINUTES

1/4 small pineapple or 2 rounds of tinned
    pineapple
1 peach
1 banana
16 strawberries
cream or yoghurt, to serve (optional)

HONEY CARDAMOM SYRUP
2 tablespoons honey
20 g (3/4 oz) unsalted butter, melted
1/2 teaspoon ground cardamom
1 tablespoon rum or brandy (optional)
1 tablespoon soft brown sugar

Soak eight wooden skewers in cold water for 30 minutes to prevent them burning during cooking. Cut the pineapple into eight bite-sized pieces. Cut the peach into eight wedges and slice the banana. Thread the fruit alternately on skewers and place in a shallow dish.

To make the honey cardamom syrup, combine all the ingredients in a bowl. Pour the mixture over the kebabs and brush to coat. Cover and leave to stand at room temperature for 1 hour. Prepare and heat a barbecue or grill (broiler).

Cook the kebabs on the hot, lightly greased barbecue or under the grill for 5 minutes. Brush with the syrup occasionally during cooking. Serve drizzled with the remaining syrup, and cream or yoghurt, if desired.

Strawberries Romanoff

Chilled Lime Soufflé

🌲 SERVES 4
🌲 PREPARATION TIME: 35 MINUTES +
🌲 COOKING TIME: 5 MINUTES

melted butter
caster (superfine) sugar, to coat
5 eggs, separated
230 g (8 oz/1 cup) caster (superfine)
    sugar
2 teaspoons finely grated lime zest
185 ml (6 fl oz/$^3/_4$ cup) lime juice,
    strained
1 tablespoon powdered gelatine
310 ml (10$^3/_4$ fl oz/1$^1/_4$ cups) whipping
    cream

Cut four strips of baking paper or foil long enough to fit around 250 ml (9 fl oz/1 cup) soufflé dishes or ramekins. Fold each in half lengthways, wrap one around each dish, extending 4 cm (1$^1/_2$ inches) above the rim, then secure with string. Brush the inside of the collar with melted butter, sprinkle with caster sugar, shake to coat, then tip out the excess.

Using electric beaters, beat the egg yolks, sugar and lime zest in a small bowl for 3 minutes, or until the sugar has dissolved and the mixture is thick and pale. Heat the lime juice in a small saucepan, then gradually add the lime juice to the yolk mixture while beating, until well mixed.

Pour 60 ml (2 fl oz/$^1/_4$ cup) water into a small heatproof bowl, sprinkle the gelatine in an even layer over the surface and leave to go spongy. Bring a large saucepan filled with 4 cm (1$^1/_2$ inches) water to the boil, remove from the heat and carefully lower the gelatine bowl into the water (it should come halfway up the side of the bowl). Stir until dissolved. Cool slightly, then add gradually to the lime mixture, beating on low speed until combined. Transfer to a large bowl, cover with plastic wrap and refrigerate for 15 minutes, or until thickened but not set.

In a small bowl, lightly whip the cream. Using a metal spoon, fold the cream into the lime mixture until almost combined.

Using electric beaters, beat the egg whites in a clean, dry bowl until soft peaks form. Fold the egg white quickly and lightly into the lime mixture, using a large metal spoon, until just combined with no lumps of egg white remaining. Spoon gently into the soufflé dishes and chill until set. Just before serving, remove the collars and serve topped with grated lime zest or whipped cream, if desired.

Chocolate Pots

🔺 SERVES 8
🔺 PREPARATION TIME: 20 MINUTES +
🔺 COOKING TIME: 1 HOUR

melted butter
170 ml (5$\frac{1}{2}$ fl oz/$\frac{2}{3}$ cup) thick
    (double/heavy) cream
$\frac{1}{2}$ vanilla bean, split lengthways
150 g (5$\frac{1}{2}$ oz) good-quality dark
    chocolate, chopped
80 ml (2$\frac{1}{2}$ fl oz/$\frac{1}{3}$ cup) milk
2 egg yolks
55 g (2 oz/$\frac{1}{4}$ cup) caster (superfine)
    sugar
whipped cream, to serve
unsweetened cocoa powder, to serve

Lightly brush eight 80 ml (2$\frac{1}{2}$ fl oz/$\frac{1}{3}$ cup) ramekins or dariole moulds with melted butter and put in a deep ovenproof dish. Preheat the oven to 140°C (275°F/Gas 1). Heat the cream and vanilla bean in a small saucepan until the cream is warm. Leave to infuse. Combine the chocolate and milk in a small saucepan. Stir constantly over low heat until the chocolate has just melted.

Put the egg yolks in a small bowl and slowly whisk in the sugar until it has dissolved and the mixture is light and creamy. Scrape the seeds out of the vanilla bean into the cream and discard the bean. Add the vanilla cream and the melted chocolate mixture to the beaten egg yolks and mix well.

Pour the mixture into the ramekins, filling about two-thirds of the way. Fill the ovenproof dish with enough boiling water to come halfway up the ramekins. Bake for 45 minutes, or until the pots have puffed up slightly and feel spongy. Remove from the dish and cool. Cover and refrigerate for 6 hours before serving. Serve with cream and a sprinkle of sifted cocoa powder.

Espresso Granita

🔺 SERVES 6
🔺 PREPARATION TIME: 10 MINUTES +
🔺 COOKING TIME: NIL

2 tablespoons caster (superfine) sugar
500 ml (17 fl oz/2 cups) hot espresso
    coffee
lightly whipped cream, to serve

Dissolve the sugar in the coffee and stir thoroughly until dissolved. Pour into a shallow metal container or tray and cool completely. Freeze for 30 minutes, then scrape with a fork to distribute the ice crystals evenly. Freeze again for 30 minutes.

Using a fork, scrape the granita into fine crystals and return to the freezer for 1 hour before serving. Spoon into glasses and top with a dollop of lightly whipped cream.

NOTE: Use a shallow tray and break the granita up when partially frozen. It is difficult to break up if made in a deep container.

Chocolate Pots

Zuccotto

1 ready-made sponge cake
80 ml (2½ fl oz/⅓ cup) Kirsch
60 ml (2 fl oz/¼ cup) Cointreau
80 ml (2½ fl oz/⅓ cup) rum, Cognac,
     Grand Marnier or Maraschino
500 ml (17 fl oz/2 cups) whipping cream
90 g (3¼ oz) dark roasted almond
     chocolate, chopped
175 g (6 oz) finely chopped mixed
     glacé fruit
100 g (3½ oz) dark chocolate, melted
70 g (2½ oz) hazelnuts, roasted
     and chopped
unsweetened cocoa powder, to decorate
icing (confectioners') sugar, to decorate

Line a 1.5 litre (52 fl oz/6 cup) pudding basin (mould) with damp muslin (cheesecloth). Cut the cake into triangular curved pieces with a knife (you will need about 12 pieces). Work with one strip of cake at a time, brushing it with the combined liqueurs and arranging the pieces closely in the basin. Put the thin ends in the centre so the slices cover the base and side of the basin. Brush with the remaining liqueur to soak the cake. Chill.

Beat the cream until stiff peaks form, then divide in half. Fold the almond chocolate and glacé fruit into one half and spread evenly over the cake in the basin, leaving a space in the centre.

Fold the cooled melted chocolate and hazelnuts into the remaining cream and spoon into the centre cavity, packing it in firmly. Smooth the surface, cover with a tea towel and chill for 8 hours to allow the cream to firm slightly. Turn out onto a plate and dust with cocoa powder and icing sugar.

Orange Sorbet

△ SERVES 6
△ PREPARATION TIME: 20 MINUTES +
△ COOKING TIME: NIL

10–12 oranges
90 g (3¼ oz/³⁄₂ cup) icing
    (confectioners') sugar
2 teaspoons lemon juice

Cut the oranges in half and carefully squeeze out the juice, taking care not to damage the skins. Dissolve the icing sugar in the orange juice, add the lemon juice and pour into a metal freezer container. Cover the surface with baking paper and freeze for 1 hour.

Scrape the remaining flesh and membrane out of six of the orange halves, cover them with plastic wrap and refrigerate.

After 1 hour, stir any frozen juice that has formed around the edge of the sorbet into the centre and return to the freezer. Repeat every hour, or until nearly frozen. Freeze overnight.

Divide the sorbet among the orange cups and freeze until ready to serve. This sorbet may seem very hard after it has frozen overnight but it will melt quickly, so work fast.

Melon Medley

△ SERVES 4
△ PREPARATION TIME: 10 MINUTES +
△ COOKING TIME: NIL

½ rockmelon or any orange-fleshed
    melon
½ honeydew melon
¼ watermelon
pulp from 2 passionfruit

Cut the melons into bite-sized pieces or use a melon baller to scoop the flesh into balls. Chill, covered, for 30 minutes. Divide among serving bowls and drizzle with the passionfruit.

Orange Sorbet

Hazelnut Torte

🌲 SERVES 8–10
🌲 PREPARATION TIME: 1 HOUR
🌲 COOKING TIME: 35 MINUTES

6 egg whites
280 g (10 oz/1¼ cups) caster (superfine)
   sugar
180 g (6½ oz) ground hazelnuts
2 tablespoons plain (all-purpose) flour,
   sifted
100 ml (3½ fl oz) white rum
chopped roasted hazelnuts, to decorate

CHOCOLATE LEAVES
150 g (5½ oz) white chocolate, chopped
non-toxic leaves (choose leaves with
   prominent veins)

WHITE CHOCOLATE CREAM
125 g (4½ oz) white chocolate, chopped
435 ml (15¼ fl oz/1¾ cups) whipping
   cream

DARK CHOCOLATE CREAM
40 g (1½ oz) dark chocolate, chopped
125 ml (4 fl oz/½ cup) whipping cream

Lightly grease two 20 cm (8 inch) round cake tins. Line the bases with baking paper and then grease the paper. Dust the tins lightly with flour, shaking off any excess. Preheat the oven to 180°C (350°F/Gas 4).

Beat the egg whites in a clean, dry bowl with electric beaters until stiff peaks form. Gradually add the sugar, beating until thick and glossy. Lightly fold in the ground hazelnuts and flour. Divide the mixture evenly between the prepared tins and smooth the tops with wet fingers. Bake for 15–20 minutes, or until the cakes feel spongy to the touch. Leave in the tins to cool a little. Cut each cake in half horizontally with a long serrated knife.

To make the chocolate leaves, put the white chocolate in a heatproof bowl. Half-fill a saucepan with water and bring to the boil, then remove the pan from the heat. Sit the bowl over the pan, making sure the base of the bowl doesn't touch the water. Stir occasionally until the chocolate has melted. Use a fine brush to paint the chocolate over the underside of the leaves. Leave to set, then peel away the leaf. If the coating of chocolate is too thin, it will break when the leaf is removed.

To make the white chocolate cream, put the chocolate in a heatproof bowl. Half-fill a saucepan with water and bring to the boil, then remove the pan from the heat. Sit the bowl over the pan, making sure the base of the bowl doesn't touch the water. Stir occasionally until the chocolate melts, then allow to cool. Whip the cream in a bowl with electric beaters until it begins to hold its shape. Add the chocolate and beat it in, then allow to cool. Make the dark chocolate cream in the same way.

Put a layer of cake on a serving plate, brush the cut surface with a little rum and spread with a quarter of the white chocolate cream. Top with a second layer of cake. Brush with rum and spread with all the dark chocolate cream. Add another layer and spread with rum and a quarter of the white chocolate cream. Top with the final layer and spread the remaining white chocolate cream over the top and side of the cake. Decorate the torte with the chopped hazelnuts and chocolate leaves.

Summer Berries in Champagne Jelly

⚜ SERVES 8

⚜ PREPARATION TIME: 10 MINUTES +

⚜ COOKING TIME: 5 MINUTES

1 litre (35 fl oz/4 cups) Champagne
    or sparkling white wine
1 1/2 tablespoons powdered gelatine
250 g (9 oz/1 cup) sugar
4 strips lemon zest
4 strips orange zest
250 g (9 oz/1 2/3 cups) small strawberries,
    hulled
250 g (9 oz/1 2/3 cups) blueberries

Pour half the Champagne into a bowl and let the bubbles subside. Sprinkle the gelatine over the top in an even layer. Leave until the gelatine is spongy — do not stir. Pour the remaining Champagne into a large saucepan, add the sugar and zests and heat gently, stirring constantly, until all the sugar has dissolved.

Remove the saucepan from the heat, add the gelatine mixture and stir until thoroughly dissolved. Leave to cool completely, then remove the zest.

Divide the berries among eight 125 ml (4 fl oz/1/2 cup) stemmed wine glasses and gently pour the jelly over them. Refrigerate until set. Remove from the refrigerator 15 minutes before serving.

Almond Jelly

⋔ PREPARATION TIME: 5 MINUTES +
⋔ COOKING TIME: 5 MINUTES

80 g (2³/₄ oz/¹/₃ cup) caster (superfine)
   sugar
2 teaspoons agar-agar (see Note)
170 ml (5¹/₂ fl oz/²/₃ cup) evaporated milk
¹/₂ teaspoon natural almond extract
3 fresh mandarins, peeled and segmented,
   or 300 g (10¹/₂ oz) fresh cherries,
   pitted and chilled

Put 500 ml (17 fl oz/2 cups) cold water and the sugar in a small saucepan. Sprinkle over the agar-agar. Bring the mixture to the boil and simmer for about 1 minute. Remove from the heat and add the evaporated milk and natural almond extract.

Pour the mixture into a shallow 18 x 28 cm (7 x 11¹/₂ inch) cake tin to set. Chill for at least 1 hour. Cut the jelly into diamond shapes, and serve with the fruit.

NOTE: Agar-agar is similar to gelatine but does not need refrigeration to help it set. If it is unavailable, use 3 teaspoons of powdered gelatine sprinkled over 125 ml (4 fl oz/¹/₂ cup) cold water to soften. Stir the gelatine mixture into the water and sugar mixture, bring to the boil, then remove it from the heat – there is no need to simmer. Proceed with the method as above but refrigerate the jelly for 5 hours instead.

Black Forest Gâteau

🔺 SERVES 8–10
🔺 PREPARATION TIME: 1 HOUR +
🔺 COOKING TIME: 1 HOUR

125 g (4½ oz) unsalted butter
230 g (8½ oz/1 cup) caster (superfine)
    sugar
2 eggs, lightly beaten
1 teaspoon natural vanilla extract
40 g (1½ oz/⅓ cup) self-raising flour
125 g (4½ oz/1 cup) plain
    (all-purpose) flour
1 teaspoon bicarbonate of soda
    (baking soda)
60 g (2¼ oz/½ cup) unsweetened
    cocoa powder
185 ml (6 fl oz/¾ cup) buttermilk
fresh or maraschino cherries with stalks,
    to decorate

TOPPING
100 g (3½ oz) dark chocolate
100 g (3½ oz) milk chocolate

FILLING
60 ml (2 fl oz/¼ cup) Kirsch
750 ml (26 fl oz/3 cups) whipping cream,
    whipped
425 g (15 oz) tinned pitted morello
    or black cherries, drained

Preheat the oven to 180°C (350°F/Gas 4). Lightly grease a deep 20 cm (8 inch) round cake tin. Line the base and side with baking paper. Using electric beaters, beat the butter and sugar until light and creamy. Add the egg gradually, beating thoroughly after each addition. Add the vanilla and beat until well combined. Transfer to a large bowl. Using a metal spoon, fold in the sifted flours, bicarbonate of soda and cocoa alternately with the buttermilk. Mix until combined and the mixture is smooth.

Pour the mixture into the tin and smooth the surface. Bake the cake for 50–60 minutes, or until a skewer inserted into the centre of the cake comes out clean. Leave the cake in the tin for 30 minutes before turning out onto a wire rack to cool. When cold, cut horizontally into three layers, using a long serrated knife. The easiest way to do this is to rest the palm of one hand lightly on top of the cake while cutting into it. Turn the cake every few strokes so the knife cuts in evenly all the way around the edge. When you have gone the whole way round, cut through the middle. Remove the first layer so it will be easier to see what you are doing while cutting the next one.

To make the topping, leave the chocolate in a warm place for 10–15 minutes, or until soft but still firm. With a vegetable peeler, and using long strokes, shave curls of chocolate from the side of the block. If the block is too soft, chill it to firm it up.

To assemble, place one cake layer on a serving plate and brush liberally with Kirsch. Spread evenly with one-fifth of the whipped cream. Top with half the cherries. Continue layering with the remaining cake, liqueur, cream and cherries, finishing with the cream on top. Spread the cream evenly on the outside of the cake. Coat the side with chocolate shavings by laying the shavings on a small piece of baking paper and then gently pressing them into the cream. If you use your hands, they will melt, so the paper acts as a barrier. Decorate the top of the cake with more chocolate shavings and fresh or maraschino cherries on stalks.

Ice Cream Cassata

⚜ SERVES 10

⚜ PREPARATION TIME: 50 MINUTES +

⚜ COOKING TIME: NIL

FIRST LAYER

2 eggs, separated
40 g (1½ oz/⅓ cup) icing
    (confectioners') sugar
185 ml (6 fl oz/¾ cup) whipping cream
50 g (1¾ oz) flaked almonds, toasted

SECOND LAYER

130 g (4¾ oz) dark chocolate, chopped
1 tablespoon dark unsweetened
    cocoa powder
2 eggs, separated
40 g (1½ oz/⅓ cup) icing
    (confectioners') sugar
185 ml (6 fl oz/¾ cup) whipping cream

THIRD LAYER

2 eggs, separated
30 g (1 oz/¼ cup) icing (confectioners')
    sugar
60 ml (2 fl oz/¼ cup) whipping cream
125 g (4½ oz/½ cup) ricotta cheese
250 g (9 oz) glacé fruit (pineapple,
    apricot, cherries, fig and peach),
    finely chopped
1 teaspoon natural vanilla extract

Line the base and sides of a deep 20 cm (8 inch) square tin with foil.

To make the first layer, beat the egg whites with electric beaters until soft peaks form. Add the icing sugar gradually, beating well after each addition. In a separate bowl, beat the cream until firm peaks form. Using a metal spoon, fold the yolks and beaten egg whites into the cream. Stir in the almonds. Spoon into the tin and smooth the surface. Tap the tin gently on the bench to level the surface, then freeze for 30–60 minutes, or until firm.

To make the second layer, put the dark chocolate in a heatproof bowl. Half-fill a saucepan with water and bring to the boil, then remove the pan from the heat. Sit the bowl over the pan, making sure the base of the bowl does not touch the water. Stir in the cocoa until smooth. Cool slightly, then proceed as for step 1, beating the egg whites and icing sugar and then the cream. Using a metal spoon, fold the chocolate into the cream. Fold in the yolks and beaten egg whites and stir until smooth. Spoon over the frozen first layer. Tap the tin on the bench to smooth the surface. Freeze for 30–60 minutes, or until firm.

To make the third layer, proceed as for the first layer, beating the egg whites with the icing sugar and then the cream. Stir the ricotta into the cream. With a metal spoon, fold the yolks and egg white into the cream, then stir in the fruit and vanilla extract. Spoon over the chocolate layer, cover the surface with baking paper, then freeze overnight. Slice to serve.

Summer Pudding

⋏ SERVES 6

⋏ PREPARATION TIME: 30 MINUTES +

⋏ COOKING TIME: 5 MINUTES

150 g (5½ oz) blackcurrants

150 g (5½ oz) redcurrants

150 g (5½ oz) raspberries

150 g (5½ oz) blackberries

200 g (7 oz) strawberries, hulled and
  quartered or halved

125 g (4½ oz/½ cup) caster (superfine)
  sugar, or to taste

6–8 slices good-quality sliced white bread,
  crusts removed

Put all the berries, except the strawberries, in a saucepan with 125 ml (4 fl oz/½ cup) water and heat for 5 minutes, or until the berries begin to collapse. Add the strawberries and remove from the heat. Add the sugar, to taste. Allow to cool.

Line a 1 litre (35 fl oz/4 cup) pudding basin (mould) or six 170 ml (5½ oz/²/₃ cup) individual moulds with the bread. For the pudding mould, cut a large circle out of one slice for the base and cut the rest of the bread into wide fingers. For the small moulds, use one slice of bread for each, cutting a small circle to fit the base and strips to fit snugly around the sides. Drain a little of the juice from the fruit mixture. Dip one side of each piece of bread in the juice before fitting it, juice side down, into the basin, leaving no gaps. Do not squeeze or flatten the bread or it will not absorb the juices. Fill the centre of the basin with the fruit and add a little juice. Cover the top with the remaining dipped bread, juice side up, trimmed to fit. Cover with plastic wrap. Place a small plate, which fits inside the dish, onto the plastic wrap, then weigh it down with heavy tins or a glass bowl. Place on a baking tray to catch any juices. For the small moulds, cover with plastic wrap and sit a small tin, or a similar weight, on top of each. Refrigerate overnight. Turn out the pudding/s and serve with any leftover fruit mixture.

Panna Cotta with Ruby Sauce

🌿 SERVES 6
🌿 PREPARATION TIME: 20 MINUTES +
🌿 COOKING TIME: 20 MINUTES

750 ml (26 fl oz/3 cups) cream
3 teaspoons powdered gelatine
1 vanilla bean
80 g (2¾ oz/⅓ cup) caster (superfine)
    sugar

RUBY SAUCE
230 g (8½ oz/1 cup) caster (superfine)
    sugar
1 cinnamon stick
125 g (4½ oz) fresh or frozen
    raspberries, plus extra, to serve
125 ml (4 fl oz/½ cup) red wine

Lightly grease six 150 ml (5 fl oz) ramekins or moulds with oil. Place 60 ml (2 fl oz/¼ cup) of the cream in a small bowl, sprinkle the gelatine in an even layer over the surface and leave to go spongy.

Put the remaining cream in a saucepan with the vanilla bean and sugar and heat gently while stirring. Remove from the heat. Whisk the gelatine into the cream mixture. Pour into the moulds and chill for 2 hours, or until set. Unmould by wiping a cloth dipped in hot water over the mould and upending it onto a plate.

While the panna cotta is chilling, make the ruby sauce. Stir the sugar with 250 ml (9 fl oz/1 cup) water in a saucepan over medium heat until the sugar has dissolved. Add the cinnamon stick and simmer for 5 minutes. Add the raspberries and wine and boil rapidly for 5 minutes. Remove the cinnamon stick and push the sauce through a sieve. Discard the seeds. Cool, then chill before serving with the panna cotta. Serve with extra raspberries.

Bellini Sorbet

🌿 SERVES 6
🌿 PREPARATION TIME: 20 MINUTES +
🌿 COOKING TIME: 25 MINUTES

460 g (1 lb/2 cups) caster (superfine)
    sugar
5 large peaches
185 ml (6 fl oz/¾ cup) Champagne
2 egg whites, lightly beaten

Combine the sugar with 1 litre (35 fl oz/4 cups) water in a large saucepan and stir over low heat until the sugar has dissolved. Bring to the boil, add the peaches and simmer for 20 minutes. Remove the peaches and cool. Reserve 250 ml (9 fl oz/1 cup) of the poaching liquid.

Peel the peaches, remove the stones and cut the flesh into chunks. Chop in a food processor until smooth, add the reserved liquid and the Champagne and process briefly until combined. Pour into a shallow metal tray and freeze for about 6 hours, until just firm. Transfer to a large bowl and beat until smooth using electric beaters. Refreeze and repeat this step twice more, adding the egg white on the final beating. Place in a storage container, cover the surface with baking paper and freeze until firm. Serve the sorbet in scoops.

Panna Cotta with Ruby Sauce

Chocolate Hazelnut Torte

⚜ SERVES 10
⚜ PREPARATION TIME: 1 HOUR +
⚜ COOKING TIME: 1 HOUR 15 MINUTES

500 g (1 lb 2 oz) dark chocolate, chopped
6 eggs
2 tablespoons Frangelico
165 g (5½ oz/1½ cups) ground hazelnuts
250 ml (9 fl oz/1 cup) whipping cream
12 whole hazelnuts, lightly roasted

CHOCOLATE TOPPING
200 g (7 oz) dark chocolate, chopped
185 ml (6 fl oz/¾ cup) cream
1 tablespoon Frangelico

Preheat the oven to 150°C (300°F/Gas 2). Grease a deep 20 cm (8 inch) round cake tin and line with baking paper.

Put the chocolate in a heatproof bowl. Half-fill a saucepan with water and bring to the boil. Remove from the heat and place the bowl over the pan, making sure it is not touching the water. Stir occasionally until the chocolate is melted. Put the eggs in a large heatproof bowl and add the Frangelico. Place the bowl over a saucepan of barely simmering water over low heat, making sure the bowl does not touch the water. Beat with an electric mixer on high speed for 7 minutes, or until the mixture is light and foamy. Remove from the heat. Using a metal spoon, quickly and lightly fold the melted chocolate and ground nuts into the egg mixture until just combined. Fold in the cream and pour the mixture into the tin. Place the tin in a shallow baking dish. Pour in enough hot water to come halfway up the side of the tin.

Bake for 1 hour, or until just set. Remove the tin from the baking dish. Cool to room temperature, cover with plastic wrap and refrigerate overnight.

Cut a 17 cm (7 inch) circle from heavy cardboard. Invert the chilled cake onto the disc so that the base of the cake becomes the top. Place on a wire rack over a baking tray and remove the baking paper. Allow the cake to return to room temperature before you start to decorate.

To make the topping, combine the chopped chocolate, cream and Frangelico in a small pan. Heat gently over low heat, stirring, until the chocolate is melted and the mixture is smooth. Pour the chocolate mixture over the cake in its centre, tilting slightly to cover the cake evenly. Tap the baking tray gently on the bench so that the top is level and the icing runs evenly over the side of the cake. Place the hazelnuts around the edge of the cake. Refrigerate just until the topping has set and the cake is firm. Carefully transfer the cake to a serving plate, and cut into thin wedges to serve.

Charlotte Malakoff

🔺 SERVES 8–12
🔺 PREPARATION TIME: 1 HOUR +
🔺 COOKING TIME: NIL

250 g (9 oz) savoiardi (lady finger)
    biscuits
125 ml (4 fl oz/^{1}/2 cup) Grand Marnier
500 g (1 lb 2 oz) strawberries, hulled and
    halved
whipped cream and strawberries,
    to decorate

ALMOND CREAM
125 g (4^1/2 oz) unsalted butter
80 g (2^3/4 oz/^{1}/3 cup) caster (superfine)
    sugar
60 ml (2 fl oz/^{1}/4 cup) Grand Marnier
^{1}/4 teaspoon natural almond extract
185 ml (6 fl oz/^{3}/4 cup) whipping cream,
    whipped
140 g (5 oz/1^1/3 cups) ground almonds

Brush a deep 1–1.5 litre (35–52 fl oz/4–6 cup) soufflé dish with melted butter or oil. Line the base with baking paper and grease the paper. Trim the biscuits to fit the height of the dish.

Combine the liqueur with 125 ml (4 fl oz/^{1}/2 cup) water. Quickly dip the biscuits into the liqueur mixture and arrange upright around the side of the dish, rounded side down.

To make the almond cream, using electric beaters, beat the butter and sugar until light and creamy. Add the liqueur and almond extract. Continue beating until the mixture is smooth and the sugar has dissolved. Using a metal spoon, fold in the whipped cream and ground almonds.

Place the strawberry halves, cut side down, into the base of the dish. Spoon one-third of the almond cream over the strawberries. Top with a layer of dipped biscuits. Continue layering, finishing with a layer of biscuits, then press down.

Cover with foil and place a small plate and weight on top. Refrigerate for 8 hours, or overnight. Remove the plate and foil and turn onto a chilled serving plate. Remove the baking paper. Decorate with whipped cream and strawberries.

NOTE: This dessert is very rich and should be served after a light main course. It is also splendid to serve when you have guests for coffee and cake, rather than a meal, and is lovely for a party.

Chocolate Rum Mousse

🔺 SERVES 4
🔺 PREPARATION TIME: 20 MINUTES +
🔺 COOKING TIME: NIL

250 g (9 oz) good-quality dark chocolate,
    chopped
3 eggs
60 g (2¼ oz/¼ cup) caster (superfine)
    sugar
2 teaspoons dark rum
250 ml (9 fl oz/1 cup) whipping cream,
    whipped
whipped cream, extra, to decorate
grated dark chocolate, to decorate

Put the chocolate in a heatproof bowl. Half-fill a saucepan with water and bring to the boil. Remove from the heat and place the bowl over the pan, making sure it is not touching the water. Stir occasionally until the chocolate has melted. Leave to cool.

Using electric beaters, beat the eggs and sugar in a bowl for 5 minutes, or until the mixture is thick, pale and increased in volume. Transfer to a large bowl.

Using a metal spoon, fold the melted chocolate and the rum through the egg mixture, leave the mixture to cool, then gently fold in the lightly whipped cream until just combined.

Spoon into four 250 ml (9 fl oz/1 cup) ramekins or dessert glasses. Refrigerate for 2 hours, or until set. Serve with extra whipped cream and garnish with grated chocolate.

Chocolate Bavarois

250 g (7 oz/1⅓ cups) dark chocolate,
chopped
375 ml (13 fl oz/1½ cups) milk
4 egg yolks
80 g (2¾ oz/⅓ cup) caster (superfine)
sugar
1 tablespoon powdered gelatine
315 ml (10¾ fl oz/1¼ cups) whipping
cream

Combine the chocolate and milk in a small saucepan. Stir over low heat until the chocolate has melted and the milk just comes to the boil. Remove from the heat.

Beat the egg yolks and sugar until combined, then gradually add the hot chocolate milk, whisking until combined. Return to a clean saucepan and cook over low heat until the mixture thickens enough to coat the back of a wooden spoon. Do not allow it to boil. Remove from the heat.

Put 2 tablespoons water in a small heatproof bowl, sprinkle the gelatine in an even layer over the surface and leave to go spongy. Stir into the hot chocolate mixture until dissolved. Refrigerate until the mixture is cold but not set, stirring occasionally.

Beat the cream until soft peaks form, then fold into the chocolate mixture in two batches. Pour into six 250 ml (9 fl oz/1 cup) glasses and refrigerate for several hours or overnight, or until set.

Fresh Fruit Pavlova

🌲 SERVES 6–8
🌲 PREPARATION TIME: 30 MINUTES
🌲 COOKING TIME: 55 MINUTES

6 egg whites
500 g (1 lb 2 oz/2⅓ cups) caster
   (superfine) sugar
1½ tablespoons cornflour (cornstarch)
1½ teaspoons vinegar
500 ml (17 fl oz/2 cups) whipping cream,
   whipped
2 bananas, sliced
500 g (1 lb 2 oz) strawberries, sliced
4 kiwi fruit, sliced
4 passionfruit, pulp removed

Preheat the oven to 150°C (300°F/Gas 2). Line a large baking tray with baking paper and draw a 26 cm (10½ inch) circle on the paper. Turn the paper over and place on the tray. Beat the egg whites with electric beaters in a large dry bowl until soft peaks form. Gradually add all but 2 tablespoons of the sugar, beating well after each addition. Combine the cornflour and vinegar with the 2 tablespoons of sugar and beat for 1 minute before adding it to the bowl. Beat for 5–10 minutes, or until all the sugar has dissolved and the meringue is stiff and glossy. Spread onto the paper inside the circle. Shape the meringue evenly, running the flat side of a palette knife along the edge and over the top.

Bake for 40 minutes, or until pale and crisp. Reduce the heat to 120°C (235°F/Gas 1–2) and bake for 15 minutes. Turn off the oven and cool the pavlova in the oven, keeping the door slightly ajar. When cooled, top with whipped cream and fruit. Drizzle with passionfruit pulp and serve.

10 eggs.

750g Sugar: 1½lb sugar

2¼ tablespn Cornflour.

2¼ " Vinegar

150.   50 mins – 60 mins

120.   30 mins.

Lemon Passionfruit Syllabub with Berries

SERVES 8–10
PREPARATION TIME: 40 MINUTES +
COOKING TIME: NIL

2 teaspoons finely grated lemon zest
80 ml (2½ fl oz/⅓ cup) lemon juice
115 g (4 oz/½ cup) caster (superfine)
    sugar
125 ml (4 fl oz/½ cup) dry white wine
8 passionfruit
500 ml (17 fl oz/2 cups) whipping cream
500 g (1 lb 2 oz) blueberries
500 g (1 lb 2 oz) raspberries
2 tablespoons icing (confectioners') sugar
500 g (1 lb 2 oz) strawberries, halved
icing (confectioners') sugar, extra, to dust

Stir the lemon zest and juice, sugar and wine together in a bowl and set aside for 10 minutes. Cut the passionfruit in half and push the pulp through a sieve to remove the seeds. Add half the passionfruit pulp to the lemon and wine mixture.

Beat the cream with electric beaters until soft peaks form. Gradually beat in the lemon and passionfruit syrup until all the syrup is added (the mixture will have the consistency of softly whipped cream). Stir in the remaining passionfruit pulp, cover and refrigerate for 1 hour.

Combine the blueberries, raspberries and icing sugar and place in a 2.5 litre (87 fl oz/10 cup) serving bowl. Spoon the cream mixture over the top. Decorate with the strawberry halves, dust with icing sugar and serve immediately.

NOTE: This traditional British custard dessert was originally made by beating milk or cream with wine, sugar, lemon juice and possibly spices, the acid curdling and thickening the mixture. Some versions were based on cider while others were further fortified with brandy. A thinner version was made as a drink and served at festive occasions in special syllabub glasses.

Flourless Chocolate Fruit and Nut Cake

SERVES 8–10

PREPARATION TIME: 40 MINUTES +

COOKING TIME: 1 HOUR

5 egg whites
170 g (6 oz/³⁄₄ cup) caster (superfine)
    sugar
100 g (3¹⁄₂ oz) glacé apricots, chopped
100 g (3¹⁄₂ oz) glacé figs, chopped
80 g (2³⁄₄ oz) glacé ginger, chopped
250 g (9 oz) blanched almonds,
    finely chopped
250 g (9 oz) dark chocolate, chopped
60 g (2¹⁄₄ oz) dark chocolate, melted
375 ml (12 fl oz/1¹⁄₂ cups) whipping
    cream
chocolate leaves, to decorate (optional)

Preheat the oven to 150°C (300°F/Gas 2). Lightly grease a deep 24 cm (9¹⁄₂ inch) round spring-form cake tin and line the base and side with baking paper.

Beat the egg whites in a bowl using electric beaters until soft peaks form. Gradually add the sugar, beating well after each addition. Beat until the sugar has dissolved and the mixture is thick and glossy.

Using a metal spoon, fold in the glacé fruit, ginger, almonds and both the chopped and melted chocolate. Stir until just combined. Spread in the tin and bake for 1 hour, or until a skewer comes out clean when inserted in the centre. Cool in the tin for 15 minutes. Remove from the tin and cool on a wire rack.

Whip the cream in a bowl using electric beaters until stiff peaks form. Using a piping (icing) bag with a plain nozzle, pipe swirls of cream on top of the cake. Decorate with chocolate leaves, if desired.

Tropical Fruit Platter

⚘ SERVES 4–6

⚘ PREPARATION TIME: 15 MINUTES

⚘ COOKING TIME: 5 MINUTES

1 lemongrass stem, white part only,
    chopped
2 cm (³/₄ inch) piece fresh ginger,
    roughly chopped
1 teaspoon soft brown sugar
125 ml (4 fl oz/¹/₂ cup) coconut milk
2 mangoes
1 nashi pear, quartered
6 lychees or rambutans, halved and
    stones removed
¹/₂ pawpaw, seeded and cut into wedges
¹/₂ red papaya, seeded and cut into wedges
2 star fruit, thickly sliced
1 lime, quartered

Simmer the lemongrass, ginger, sugar and coconut milk in a small saucepan over low heat for 5 minutes. Strain and set aside.

Cut down both sides of the mangoes close to the stones. Score a crisscross pattern into each half, without cutting through the skin. Fold the outer edges under, pushing the centre up from underneath. Arrange with the rest of the fruit on a platter. Add the lime, for squeezing on the fruit.

Serve the coconut dressing on the side as a dipping sauce or drizzle over just before serving.

Summer Fruit Compote

⚘ SERVES 8

⚘ PREPARATION TIME: 40 MINUTES

⚘ COOKING TIME: 30 MINUTES

5 apricots, halved
4 nectarines, halved
4 blood plums or other plums, stoned
4 peaches, quartered
200 g (7 oz) tinned pitted cherries
250 ml (9 fl oz/1 cup) claret
80 ml (2¹/₂ fl oz/¹/₃ cup) dry sherry
170 g (6 oz/³/₄ cup) caster (superfine)
    sugar
whipped cream, to serve (optional)

Gently plunge the fruit in small batches into boiling water for 30 seconds. Remove and put in a bowl of iced water. Peel all the fruit except the cherries.

Combine the claret, sherry, sugar and 250 ml (9 fl oz/ 1 cup) water in a large heavy-based saucepan. Stir over low heat without boiling until the sugar has dissolved. Bring to the boil, reduce the heat and simmer for 5 minutes.

Add the drained fruits to the syrup in small batches and simmer each batch for 5 minutes. Remove with a slotted spoon. Pile the fruit into a bowl. Bring the syrup to the boil, reduce the heat and simmer for a further 5 minutes. Remove from the heat and allow to cool slightly — it should be the consistency of a syrup. Pour over the fruit. Serve with a dollop of freshly whipped cream.

Tropical Fruit Platter

Orange and Lemon Syrup Cake

🌿 SERVES 10–12

🌿 PREPARATION TIME: 40 MINUTES

🌿 COOKING TIME: 1 HOUR

BUTTER CAKE

185 g (6½ oz/1½ cups) self-raising flour

60 g (2¼ oz/½ cup) plain (all-purpose) flour

185 g (6½ oz) unsalted butter, chopped and softened

170 g (6 oz/¾ cup) caster (superfine) sugar

3 eggs, lightly beaten

1 teaspoon natural vanilla extract

1 teaspoon grated orange zest

60 ml (2 fl oz/¼ cup) milk

SYRUP

2 oranges

2 lemons

520 g (1 lb 2½ oz/2¼ cups) caster (superfine) sugar

Preheat the oven to 180°C (350°F/Gas 4). Lightly grease a 20 cm (8 inch) kugelhopf tin. Dust lightly with flour.

Sift the flours into a bowl. Cream the butter and sugar in a small bowl using electric beaters until light and fluffy. With the beaters still running, add the egg gradually, a little at a time, beating thoroughly after each addition. Add the vanilla and beat well to combine. Transfer the mixture to a large bowl and, using a large metal spoon, gently fold in the sifted flour, orange zest and milk. Stir until just combined and almost smooth. Spoon the mixture into the tin and cook for 1 hour, or until a skewer inserted into the centre of the cake comes out clean.

Cut the oranges and lemons into thin slices, without peeling them. To make the syrup, place 250 g (9 oz/ 1 cup) of the sugar in a heavy-based frying pan with 80 ml (2½ fl oz/⅓ cup) water. Stir over low heat until the sugar has completely dissolved. Bring to the boil, then reduce the heat and simmer. Add a quarter of the sliced fruit to the syrup and leave to simmer for 5–10 minutes, or until transparent and toffee-like. Lift out the fruit with tongs and cool on a wire rack. Add an extra 90 g (3¼ oz/⅓ cup) of sugar to the syrup and stir gently to dissolve — the juice from the fruit breaks down the concentrated syrup and the fruit won't candy properly unless you add the sugar. Simmer the second batch of sliced fruit. Add 90 g (3¼ oz/⅓ cup) of sugar to the syrup before cooking each batch.

When all the fruit has been candied, turn the cake out onto a wire rack over a tray and pour the hot syrup over the warm cake, allowing it to soak in — if the syrup is too thick, thin it with a little orange juice. Put the cake on a serving plate. When the fruit slices have firmed, arrange them on top of the cake (you can cut and twist some of the slices).

Green Tea Ice Cream

🌲 SERVES 4
🌲 PREPARATION TIME: 15 MINUTES +
🌲 COOKING TIME: 30 MINUTES

4 tablespoons Japanese green tea leaves
500 ml (17 fl oz/2 cups) milk
6 egg yolks
115 g (4 oz/½ cup) caster (superfine)
    sugar
500 ml (17 fl oz/2 cups) cream

Combine the green tea leaves with the milk in a saucepan and slowly bring to simmering point. This step should not be rushed – the longer the milk takes to come to a simmer, the better the infusion of flavour. Set aside for 5 minutes before straining.

Whisk the egg yolks and sugar in a heatproof bowl until thick and pale, then add the infused milk. Place the bowl over a saucepan of simmering water, making sure that the base of the bowl does not touch the water. Stir the custard until it is thick enough to coat the back of the spoon, then remove from the heat and allow to cool slightly before stirring through the cream. Transfer to an ice cream machine and freeze according to the manufacturer's instructions. Alternatively, transfer to a shallow metal tray and freeze, whisking every couple of hours until frozen and creamy. Freeze overnight.

NOTE: If you prefer your green tea ice cream pale green, add a few drops of green food colouring.

Mango Fool

🌲 SERVES 6
🌲 PREPARATION TIME: 20 MINUTES + CHILLING
🌲 COOKING TIME: NIL

3 large mangoes
250 ml (8 fl oz/1 cup) ready-made
    custard
420 ml (14½ fl oz/1⅔ cups) whipping
    cream

Peel and stone the mangoes and purée the flesh in a food processor. Add the custard and blend to combine.

Whip the cream until soft peaks form, then gently fold into the mango mixture until just combined – do not overmix, as you want to end up with a decorative marbled effect.

Pour the mixture into a serving dish or individual glasses. Gently smooth the top, then refrigerate for at least 1 hour before serving. Serve with fresh fruit, if desired.

Green Tea Ice Cream

Cranachan

SERVES 6

PREPARATION TIME: 30 MINUTES +

COOKING TIME: 10 MINUTES

2 tablespoons oatmeal
250 ml (9 fl oz/1 cup) whipping cream
2 tablespoons honey
1 tablespoon whisky
500 g (1 lb 2 oz) raspberries or
    strawberries, plus extra berries to
    decorate
2 tablespoons rolled (porridge) oats,
    toasted

Put the oatmeal in a small frying pan. Stir over low heat for 5 minutes, or until lightly toasted. Remove from the heat and cool completely.

Using electric beaters, beat the cream in a small bowl until soft peaks form. Add the honey and whisky and beat until just combined. Fold the cooled, toasted oatmeal into the cream mixture with a metal spoon.

Alternately, layer the berries and cream into six tall dessert glasses, finishing with the cream. Refrigerate for 2 hours and serve sprinkled with toasted oats and a few final berries.

NOTE: In Scotland, charms are placed into cranachan at Halloween, somewhat like the customary coins in English Christmas puddings.

Zuppa Inglese

500 ml (17 fl oz/2 cups) milk
1 vanilla bean, split lengthways
4 egg yolks
115 g (4 oz/$\frac{1}{2}$ cup) caster (superfine)
   sugar
2 tablespoons plain (all-purpose) flour
300 g (10$\frac{1}{2}$ oz) Madeira cake, cut into
   1 cm ($\frac{1}{2}$ inch) thick slices
80 ml (2$\frac{1}{2}$ fl oz/$\frac{1}{3}$ cup) rum
30 g (1 oz) chocolate, grated or shaved
50 g (1$\frac{3}{4}$ oz) flaked almonds, toasted

Heat the milk and vanilla bean in a saucepan over low heat until bubbles appear around the edge of the pan.

Whisk the egg yolks, sugar and flour together in a bowl until thick and pale.

Discard the vanilla bean and whisk the warm milk slowly into the egg mixture, then blend well. Return to a clean saucepan and stir over medium heat until the custard boils and thickens. Allow to cool slightly.

Line the base of a 1.5 litre (52 fl oz/6 cup) serving dish with one-third of the cake slices and brush well with the rum combined with 1 tablespoon water. Spread one-third of the custard over the cake. Repeat this process, finishing with a layer of custard. Cover and refrigerate for 3 hours. Sprinkle with the chocolate and almonds just before serving.

Kulfi

1½ litres (52 fl oz/6 cups) milk
8 cardamom pods
4 tablespoons caster (superfine) sugar
20 g (¾ oz) blanched almonds,
    finely chopped
20 g (¾ oz) pistachio nuts, chopped,
    plus extra, to garnish
vegetable oil, for greasing

Put the milk and cardamom pods in a large heavy-based saucepan, bring to the boil then reduce the heat and simmer, stirring often until it has reduced by about one-third, to 1 litre (35 fl oz/4 cups) — this will take some time. Keep stirring or it will stick.

Add the sugar and cook for 2–3 minutes. Strain out the cardamom pods and add the nuts. Pour the kulfi into a shallow metal or plastic container, cover the surface with a sheet of baking paper and freeze for 1 hour. Remove from the freezer and beat to break up any ice crystals, freeze again and repeat twice more.

Lightly brush six 250 ml (9 fl oz/1 cup) pudding basins (moulds) with the oil and divide the kulfi among them, then freeze overnight. To serve, unmould each kulfi and cut a cross ½ cm (¼ inch) deep in the top. Serve with extra pistachio nuts sprinkled over the top.

Strawberries and Cream Sponge with Toffee

🌲 SERVES 10–12

🌲 PREPARATION TIME: 40 MINUTES +

🌲 COOKING TIME: 30 MINUTES

75 g (2¾ oz) plain (all-purpose) flour
150 g (5½ oz) self-raising flour
6 eggs
220 g (7¾ oz) caster (superfine) sugar
2 tablespoons boiling water
750 ml (26 fl oz/3 cups) whipping cream
2 tablespoons icing (confectioners') sugar
500 g (1 lb 2 oz/3⅓ cups) strawberries
Kirsch or Cointreau, to brush
230 g (8½ oz/1 cup) caster (superfine) sugar, extra

Preheat the oven to 180°C (350°F/Gas 4). Grease two deep 22 cm (8½ inch) round cake tins and line the bases with baking paper. Lightly dust the tins with flour, shaking off the excess. Sift the flours three times onto baking paper. Beat the eggs in a large bowl using electric beaters for 7 minutes, or until thick and pale.

Add the sugar gradually to the eggs, beating thoroughly after each addition. Using a metal spoon, fold in the sifted flour and boiling water. Spread the mixture evenly into the tins and bake for 25 minutes, or until the sponges are lightly golden and shrink slightly from the sides of the tins. Leave the sponges in their tins for 5 minutes before turning out onto a wire rack to cool.

Using a serrated knife, slice each cake horizontally in half (you will only need three layers of cake, so freeze the remaining portion for trifles or cake crumbs). Whip the cream and icing sugar into stiff peaks. Hull the strawberries and thinly slice half of them.

Place one layer of cake on a serving plate and brush with a little liqueur. Spread with one-third of the cream and scatter with half the sliced strawberries. Repeat with another layer of cake, liqueur, cream and sliced strawberries. Place the last cake layer on top and spread the remaining cream over the top. Arrange the remaining whole strawberries on top and refrigerate.

To make the toffee, put a heavy-based frying pan over medium heat, gradually sprinkle with some of the extra sugar and, as it melts, sprinkle with the remaining sugar. Stir to melt any lumps and prevent the sugar burning. When the toffee is golden brown, remove the pan from the heat. Dip two forks in the toffee, then rub the backs of the forks together until the toffee begins to stick. Gently pull the forks apart to check whether the toffee is cool enough to spin. If it drips or dips, it probably needs a little longer to cool. If not, continue pulling the toffee apart over the cake, pressing the forks together to spin a second time when they meet. Re-dip and continue spinning backwards and forwards and over the cake. Serve as soon as you've spun the toffee.

Coconut Semolina Slice

🌿 SERVES 8–10

🌿 PREPARATION TIME: 20 MINUTES

🌿 COOKING TIME: 1 HOUR

50 g (1¾ oz) white sesame seeds
125 g (4½ oz/1 cup) fine semolina
230 g (8½ oz/1 cup) caster (superfine)
    sugar
750 ml (26 fl oz/3 cups) coconut cream
2 tablespoons ghee or oil
2 eggs, separated
¼ teaspoon ground cardamom
fresh fruit, to serve (optional)

Preheat the oven to 160°C (315°F/Gas 2–3). Lightly grease a 18 x 28 cm (7 x 11 inch) shallow tin.

Toast the sesame seeds in a dry frying pan over medium heat for 3–4 minutes, shaking the pan gently, until the seeds are golden brown; remove from the pan at once to prevent burning.

Put the semolina, sugar and coconut cream in a large saucepan and stir over medium heat for 5 minutes, or until boiling. Add the ghee or oil and continue stirring until the mixture comes away from the sides of the pan. Set aside to cool.

Beat the egg whites until stiff peaks form. Fold the egg whites, egg yolks and cardamom into the cooled semolina mixture. Spoon the mixture into the prepared tin and sprinkle with the sesame seeds. Bake for 45 minutes, or until golden brown. Cut into diamond shapes and serve with fresh fruit, if desired.

Mixed Berry Meringue Stacks

SERVES 6

PREPARATION TIME: 50 MINUTES

COOKING TIME: 35 MINUTES

2 egg whites
115 g (4 oz/$\frac{1}{2}$ cup) caster (superfine)
    sugar
250 g (9 oz) strawberries
150 g (5$\frac{1}{2}$ oz) blueberries
125 g (4$\frac{1}{2}$ oz) raspberries
1 tablespoon soft brown sugar
375 ml (13 fl oz/1$\frac{1}{2}$ cups) whipping
    cream, whipped
icing (confectioners') sugar, to dust

Preheat the oven to 150°C (300°F/Gas 2). Line baking trays with baking paper and mark out eighteen 9 cm (3$\frac{1}{2}$ inch) circles.

Using electric beaters, beat the egg whites in a clean, dry large bowl until soft peaks form. Gradually add the sugar, beating after each addition, until the mixture is thick and glossy. Spread 1 tablespoon of the mixture evenly over each of the circles to a thickness of 5 mm ($\frac{1}{4}$ inch). Bake for 30–35 minutes, or until lightly golden, then turn the oven off and leave the meringues to cool completely in the oven.

Chop the strawberries and combine with the other berries in a large bowl. Sprinkle with the brown sugar, then cover and refrigerate for 20 minutes.

To assemble, using three meringue circles for each, place one on a plate, spread with whipped cream and arrange some of the berries over the cream. Place another circle on top, spread with cream, top with more berries and then top with the third circle. Dust liberally with icing sugar. Repeat this with all the circles to make six individual stacks. Serve immediately.

Almond Semifreddo

🔥 SERVES 8–10
🔥 PREPARATION TIME: 30 MINUTES +
🔥 COOKING TIME: NIL

310 ml (10¾ fl oz/1¼ cups) whipping
    cream
4 eggs, at room temperature, separated
85 g (3 oz/⅔ cup) icing
    (confectioners') sugar
60 ml (2 fl oz/¼ cup) amaretto
80 g (2¾ oz/½ cup) toasted almonds,
    chopped
8 amaretti biscuits (cookies), crushed
fresh fruit or extra amaretto, to serve

Whip the cream until firm peaks form, then cover and refrigerate. Line a 10 x 21 cm (4 x 8½ inch) loaf (bar) tin with plastic wrap so that it overhangs the two long sides.

Beat the egg yolks and icing sugar in a large bowl until pale and creamy. Whisk the egg whites in a separate bowl until firm peaks form. Stir the amaretto, almonds and amaretti biscuits into the egg yolk mixture, then carefully fold in the chilled cream and the egg whites until well combined. Carefully pour or spoon into the lined loaf tin and cover with the overhanging plastic. Freeze for 4 hours, or until frozen but not rock hard. Serve slices with fresh fruit or a sprinkling of amaretto.

NOTES: Semifreddo means semi frozen, so if you leave it in the freezer overnight, put it in the refrigerator for 30 minutes before serving. The semifreddo can also be frozen in individual moulds or serving dishes.

Figs in Honey Syrup

🔥 SERVES 4
🔥 PREPARATION TIME: 20 MINUTES
🔥 COOKING TIME: 1 HOUR

100 g (3½ oz) blanched whole almonds
12 whole fresh figs (about 750 g/
    1 lb 10 oz)
110 g (3¾ oz/½ cup) sugar
115 g (4 oz/⅓ cup) honey
2 tablespoons lemon juice
6 cm (2½ inch) piece lemon zest
1 cinnamon stick
250 g (9 oz/1 cup) Greek-style yoghurt

Preheat the oven to 180°C (350°F/Gas 4). Place the almonds on a baking tray and bake for 5 minutes, or until golden. Leave to cool. Make a small crossways incision on top of each fig. Push an almond into the base of each fig. Roughly chop the remaining almonds.

Put 750 ml (26 fl oz/3 cups) water in a large saucepan, add the sugar and stir over medium heat until the sugar dissolves. Increase the heat and bring to the boil. Stir in the honey, lemon juice, lemon zest and cinnamon stick. Reduce the heat to medium, put the figs in the pan and simmer gently for 30 minutes. Remove with a slotted spoon and place on a large serving dish.

Boil the liquid over high heat for about 15–20 minutes, or until thick and syrupy. Remove the cinnamon and lemon zest. Cool the syrup slightly and pour over the figs. Sprinkle with the chopped almonds. Serve warm or cold with the yoghurt.

Almond Semifreddo

Baked Lime and Passionfruit Cheesecake

🔺 SERVES 6–8
🔺 PREPARATION TIME: 50 MINUTES +
🔺 COOKING TIME: 55 MINUTES

250 g (9 oz) plain sweet biscuits
125 g (4½ oz) unsalted butter, melted

FILLING
500 g (1 lb 2 oz) cream cheese, softened
    to room temperature
80 g (2¾ oz/⅓ cup) caster (superfine)
    sugar
3 teaspoons finely grated lime zest
2 tablespoons lime juice
2 eggs, lightly beaten
125 g (4½ oz/½ cup) passionfruit pulp

PASSIONFRUIT TOPPING
1 tablespoon caster (superfine) sugar
3 teaspoons cornflour (cornstarch)
125 g (4½ oz/½ cup) passionfruit pulp

Lightly grease a 20 cm (8 inch) diameter spring-form cake tin and line the base with baking paper. Preheat the oven to 160°C (315°F/Gas 2–3). Finely crush the biscuits in a food processor and mix in the butter. Spoon into the tin and press firmly into the base and side of the tin. Chill for 30 minutes.

Using electric beaters, beat the cream cheese, sugar, lime zest and lime juice until creamy. Gradually beat in the eggs and passionfruit pulp. Pour into the tin, put on a baking tray to catch any drips, and bake for 45–50 minutes, or until just set. Cool completely.

To make the passionfruit topping, combine the sugar, cornflour and 2 tablespoons water in a small saucepan over low heat. Stir until smooth, then add another 2 tablespoons water and the passionfruit pulp and stir until the mixture boils and thickens. Pour the hot topping over the cooled cheesecake, spread evenly and cool completely. Refrigerate overnight. Serve with whipped cream if desired.

NOTE: You will need to use the pulp from about eight fresh passionfruit for this recipe.

Macerated Oranges

4 oranges

1 teaspoon grated lemon zest

55 g (2 oz/¼ cup) caster (superfine)
    sugar

1 tablespoon lemon juice

2 tablespoons Cointreau or Maraschino
    (optional)

Cut a thin slice off the top and bottom of the oranges. Using a small sharp knife, slice off the skin and pith, removing as much pith as possible. Slice down the side of a segment between the flesh and the membrane. Repeat on the other side and lift the segment out. Do this over a bowl to catch the juice. Repeat with all the segments. Squeeze out any juice remaining in the membranes.

Place the segments on a shallow dish and sprinkle with the lemon zest, sugar and lemon juice. Toss carefully. Cover and refrigerate for at least 2 hours. Toss again. Serve chilled. Add Cointreau or Maraschino just before serving, if desired.

Chocolate Liqueur Frappé

⚜ SERVES 2

⚜ PREPARATION TIME: 10 MINUTES

⚜ COOKING TIME: NIL

260 g (9 oz/2 cups) ice-cubes

125 ml (4 fl oz/$\frac{1}{2}$ cup) milk

60 ml (2 fl oz/$\frac{1}{4}$ cup) whipping cream

2 tablespoons Frangelico

45 g (1$\frac{1}{2}$ oz/$\frac{1}{4}$ cup) icing
     (confectioners') sugar

2 tablespoons cocoa powder, plus extra,
     to dust

Combine the ice cubes, milk, cream, Frangelico, icing sugar and cocoa powder in a blender. Blend until thick and creamy. Pour the mixture into tall glasses and serve immediately, dusted with cocoa.

NOTE: You can omit the Frangelico if you wish or even replace it with another liqueur such as Tia Maria or Kahlua.

hot desserts

Chocolate Pudding

⚘ SERVES 6
⚘ PREPARATION TIME: 20 MINUTES
⚘ COOKING TIME: 1 HOUR 15 MINUTES

125 g (4½ oz) dark chocolate, chopped
90 g (3¼ oz) unsalted butter, at room
    temperature
95 g (3¼ oz/½ cup) soft brown sugar
3 eggs, separated
1 teaspoon natural vanilla extract
125 g (4½ oz/1 cup) self-raising flour
1 tablespoon unsweetened cocoa powder
½ teaspoon bicarbonate of soda
    (baking soda)
60 ml (2 fl oz/¼ cup) milk
2 tablespoons brandy
whipped cream, to serve

CHOCOLATE SAUCE
125 g (4½ oz) dark chocolate, chopped
60 ml (2 fl oz/¼ cup) whipping cream
1 tablespoon brandy

Grease a 1.25 litre (44 fl oz/5 cup) pudding basin (mould) and line the base with a circle of baking paper. Preheat the oven to 180°C (350°F/Gas 4).

Put the chocolate in a heatproof bowl. Half-fill a saucepan with water and bring to the boil, then remove the pan from the heat. Sit the bowl over the pan, making sure the base of the bowl doesn't touch the water. Stir occasionally until the chocolate has melted. Set aside to cool. Keep the saucepan of water for later, to make the chocolate sauce.

Cream the butter and half the brown sugar until light and creamy. Beat in the egg yolks, melted chocolate and vanilla. Sift together the flour, cocoa and bicarbonate of soda. Fold into the mixture, alternating with spoonfuls of the combined milk and brandy.

Beat the egg whites in a clean, dry bowl until soft peaks form. Gradually beat in the remaining sugar, until stiff and glossy, then fold into the chocolate mixture.

Pour into the prepared basin. Cover tightly with foil and secure with string. Put in a deep ovenproof dish and pour in enough hot water to come halfway up the side of the basin. Bake for 1 hour 15 minutes, or until a skewer comes out clean. Unmould onto a plate.

To make the chocolate sauce, put the chocolate, cream and brandy in a heatproof bowl. Reheat the saucepan of water, bring to the boil, then remove the pan from the heat. Sit the bowl over the pan, making sure the base of the bowl doesn't touch the water. Stir occasionally until the chocolate has melted and the sauce is smooth. Serve the pudding with the chocolate sauce and with whipped cream.

Poached Pears with Ginger Zabaglione

🔺 MAKES 6
🔺 PREPARATION TIME: 30 MINUTES
🔺 COOKING TIME: 1 HOUR

500 ml (17 fl oz/2 cups) red wine
4 pieces crystallised ginger
110 g (3¾ oz/½ cup) sugar
6 pears, peeled

GINGER ZABAGLIONE
8 egg yolks
80 g (2¾ oz/⅓ cup) caster (superfine)
    sugar
1 teaspoon ground ginger
310 ml (10¾ fl oz/1¼ cups) Marsala

Put the wine, ginger and sugar in a large saucepan with 1 litre (35 fl oz/4 cups) water and stir over medium heat until the sugar has dissolved. Add the pears, cover and simmer for 45 minutes, or until tender.

To make the zabaglione, put a large saucepan half-filled with water on to the boil. When boiling, remove from the heat. Beat the egg yolks, sugar and ginger in a metal or heatproof bowl, using electric beaters, until pale yellow. Set the bowl over the saucepan of steaming water, making sure the base of the bowl does not touch the water, and beat continuously, adding the Marsala gradually. Beat for 5 minutes, or until very thick and foamy and mousse-like.

Remove the pears from the pan with a slotted spoon. Arrange on plates and pour the ginger zabaglione over. Serve immediately.

Sweet Won Tons

125 g (4 1/2 oz) dates, pitted and chopped
2 bananas, finely chopped
45 g (1 3/4 oz/1/2 cup) flaked almonds,
    lightly crushed
1/2 teaspoon ground cinnamon
60 won ton wrappers
oil, for deep-frying
icing (confectioners') sugar, to dust

Combine the dates, banana, almonds and cinnamon. Put 2 teaspoons of the fruit mixture into the centre of a won ton wrapper and brush the edges lightly with water. Place another won ton wrapper on top at an angle so that the wrappers make a star shape. Place the won tons on a baking tray lined with baking paper. Repeat with the remaining ingredients, taking care not to stack the won tons on top of each other or they will stick together.

Fill a deep-fryer or large heavy-based saucepan one-third full of oil and heat to 180°C (350°F), or until a cube of bread dropped into the oil browns in 15 seconds. Deep-fry the won tons, in small batches for 2 minutes, or until crisp and golden. Drain on paper towel. Dust the won tons lightly with icing sugar before serving.

White Chocolate Fondue with Fruit

🌲 SERVES 6–8
🌲 PREPARATION TIME: 15 MINUTES
🌲 COOKING TIME: 10 MINUTES

125 ml (4 fl oz/½ cup) light corn syrup
170 ml (5½ fl oz/⅔ cup) thick
   (double/heavy) cream
60 ml (2 fl oz/¼ cup) Cointreau or
   orange-flavoured liquer
250 g (9 oz) white chocolate, chopped
marshmallows and fresh fruit (such as
   sliced peaches, strawberries and
   cherries)

Combine the corn syrup and cream in a small pan or fondue pot. Bring to the boil, then remove from the heat.

Add the liqueur and white chocolate and stir until melted. Serve with marshmallows and fresh fruit.

Dark Chocolate Fondue with Fruit

🌲 SERVES 6–8
🌲 PREPARATION TIME: 30 MINUTES
🌲 COOKING TIME: 20 MINUTES

250 g (9 oz) dark chocolate, chopped
125 ml (4 fl oz/½ cup) thick
   (double/heavy) cream
marshmallows and chopped fresh fruit
   (such as strawberries, pears, cherries
   and bananas), to serve

Put the chocolate and cream in a fondue pot or a heatproof bowl. Heat gently in the fondue pot, stirring until smooth or, alternatively, place the bowl over a saucepan of water which has been brought to the boil and then taken off the heat — make sure the base of the bowl is not touching the water. Serve from the bowl or fondue pot with some marshmallows and fresh fruit for dipping.

White Chocolate Fondue with Fruit

Chocolate Mint Self-Saucing Pudding

▲ SERVES 6
▲ PREPARATION TIME: 15 MINUTES
▲ COOKING TIME: 45 MINUTES

185 ml (6 fl oz/¾ cup) milk
115 g (4 oz/½ cup) caster (superfine)
   sugar
60 g (2¼ oz) unsalted butter, melted
1 egg
125 g (4½ oz/1 cup) self-raising flour
40 g (1½ oz/⅓ cup) unsweetened cocoa
   powder
250 ml (9 fl oz/1 cup) boiling water
125 g (4½ oz) dark mint-flavoured
   chocolate, roughly chopped
230 g (8 oz/1 cup) soft brown sugar
ice cream, to serve

Preheat the oven to 180°C (350°F/Gas 4). Grease a
1.5 litre (52 fl oz/6 cup) capacity ovenproof dish.

Whisk together the milk, sugar, butter and egg in a
bowl. Sift the flour and half the cocoa powder onto the
milk mixture, add the chocolate and stir to mix well.
Pour the mixture into the dish.

Put the brown sugar and remaining cocoa powder into
a bowl and stir in boiling water. Carefully pour this
over the pudding mixture.

Bake for 40–45 minutes, or until the pudding is cooked
and is firm to the touch. Spoon over the sauce and serve
hot or warm with ice cream.

NOTE: If you prefer, substitute plain dark chocolate or another type of
flavoured chocolate (such as orange chocolate) for the mint chocolate.

Sticky Date Pudding

🍃 SERVES 6–8
🍃 PREPARATION TIME: 35 MINUTES +
🍃 COOKING TIME: 50 MINUTES

200 g (7 oz) dates, pitted and chopped
1 teaspoon bicarbonate of soda
    (baking soda)
100 g (3½ oz) unsalted butter
170 g (6 oz/¾ cup) caster (superfine)
    sugar
2 eggs, lightly beaten
1 teaspoon natural vanilla extract
185 g (6½ oz/1½ cups) self-raising flour
whipped cream and raspberries, to serve

SAUCE
185 g (6½ oz/1 cup) soft brown sugar
125 ml (4 fl oz/½ cup) cream
100 g (3½ oz) unsalted butter

Preheat the oven to 180°C (350°F/Gas 4). Lightly grease a 20 cm (8 inch) square cake tin. Line the base with baking paper. Combine the dates with 250 ml (9 fl oz/1 cup) water in a small saucepan. Bring to the boil and remove from the heat. Stir in the bicarbonate of soda and set aside to cool to room temperature.

Using electric beaters, beat the butter and sugar in a small bowl until light and creamy. Add the eggs gradually, beating thoroughly after each addition. Add the vanilla and beat until combined. Transfer to a large bowl.

Using a metal spoon, fold in the flour and dates with the liquid and stir until just combined — do not overbeat. Pour into the prepared tin and bake for 50 minutes, or until a skewer comes out clean when inserted into the centre of the pudding. Leave in the tin for 10 minutes before turning out.

To make the sauce, combine the sugar, cream and butter in a small saucepan. Stir until the butter melts and the sugar dissolves. Bring to the boil, reduce the heat and simmer for 2 minutes. Pour over slices of pudding and serve immediately, with whipped cream and raspberries.

Beignets de Fruits

🌲 SERVES 4
🌲 PREPARATION TIME: 25 MINUTES +
🌲 COOKING TIME: 10 MINUTES

3 granny smith or golden delicious apples
70 g (2½ oz) raisins
60 ml (2 fl oz/¼ cup) Calvados or rum
1½ tablespoons caster (superfine) sugar
oil, for frying
2 tablespoons plain (all-purpose) flour,
    to coat
icing (confectioners') sugar, to dust

BATTER
1 egg, separated
70 ml (2¼ fl oz) warm beer
60 g (2¼ oz/½ cup) plain (all-purpose)
    flour
1 teaspoon oil

Peel and core the apples and cut into 1 cm (½ inch) cubes. Place in a bowl with the raisins, Calvados and sugar and marinate for 3 hours.

To make the batter, beat the egg yolk and beer together in a large bowl. Blend in the flour, oil and a pinch of salt. Stir until smooth. The batter will be very thick at this stage. Cover and leave in a warm place for 1 hour.

Pour the oil into a large saucepan to a depth of 10 cm (4 inches) and heat to 170°C (325°F), or until a cube of bread dropped into the oil browns in 20 seconds. Add 1½ tablespoons of the Calvados liquid to the batter and stir until smooth. Whisk the egg white until stiff and gently fold into the batter. Drain the apples and raisins, toss with the flour to coat, then lightly fold them through the batter. Carefully lower heaped tablespoons of batter into the oil in batches and fry for 1–2 minutes, until the fritters are golden on both sides. Remove with a slotted spoon and drain on paper towel. Keep warm while you cook the remaining fritters. Dust with icing sugar and serve.

Spicy Coconut Custard

▲ SERVES 8
▲ PREPARATION TIME: 20 MINUTES
▲ COOKING TIME: 1 HOUR

2 cinnamon sticks
1 teaspoon freshly grated nutmeg
2 teaspoons whole cloves
310 ml (10¾ fl oz/1¼ cups) cream
90 g (3¼ oz) chopped palm sugar
    (jaggery), or soft brown sugar
270 ml (9½ fl oz) coconut milk
3 eggs, lightly beaten
2 egg yolks, lightly beaten
whipped cream, to serve
toasted flaked coconut, to serve

Preheat the oven to 160°C (315°F/Gas 2–3). Combine the cinnamon, nutmeg, cloves, cream and 250 ml (9 fl oz/1 cup) water in a saucepan. Bring to simmering point, reduce the heat to very low and leave for 5 minutes to allow the spices to infuse the liquid. Add the sugar and coconut milk, return to low heat and stir until the sugar has dissolved.

Whisk the eggs and egg yolks in a bowl until combined. Stir in the spiced mixture, then strain, discarding the whole spices. Pour into eight 125 ml (4 fl oz/¼ cup) ramekins or dariole moulds. Place in a baking dish and pour in enough hot water to come halfway up the sides of the ramekins. Bake for 40–45 minutes until set. The custards should wobble slightly when the dish is shaken lightly. Remove the custards from the baking dish. Serve hot or chilled with whipped cream and toasted flaked coconut sprinkled over the top.

Almond Mascarpone Crepes with Summer Fruit

🔻 MAKES ABOUT 12 CREPES
🔻 PREPARATION TIME: 40 MINUTES +
🔻 COOKING TIME: 35 MINUTES

ALMOND MASCARPONE
60 g (2¼ oz/½ cup) slivered almonds
115 g (4 oz/½ cup) caster (superfine)
    sugar
500 g (1 lb 2 oz) mascarpone cheese

250 g (9 oz) strawberries, sliced
1 tablespoon caster (superfine) sugar
125 g (4½ oz/1 cup) plain (all-purpose)
    flour
2 eggs
125 ml (4 fl oz/½ cup) milk
30 g (1 oz) unsalted butter, melted
melted butter, extra, to grease
4 kiwi fruit, thinly sliced
200 g (7 oz) raspberries
250 g (9 oz) blueberries

To make the almond mascarpone, preheat the grill (broiler) to low and grill (broil) the almonds until lightly golden, then place on a greased baking tray. Put the sugar in a small heavy-based saucepan with 125 ml (4 fl oz/½ cup) water and stir, without boiling, until the sugar has dissolved. Bring to the boil, then reduce the heat and simmer, without stirring, for 15 minutes, or until the liquid turns golden brown. Quickly pour over the almonds and leave to set. Break into chunks and finely grind in a food processor. Transfer to a bowl, stir in the mascarpone, cover and refrigerate.

Place the strawberries in a large bowl and sprinkle with the sugar. Stir to combine, then refrigerate.

Combine the flour, eggs and milk in a food processor for 10 seconds. Add 125 ml (4 fl oz/½ cup) water and the melted butter and process until smooth. Pour into a jug and set aside for 30 minutes.

Heat a small crepe pan or non-stick frying pan and brush lightly with the extra melted butter. Pour 60 ml (2 fl oz/¼ cup) batter into the pan, swirling to cover the base thinly. Cook for about 30 seconds, or until the edges just begin to curl, then turn the crepe over and cook the other side until lightly browned. Transfer to a plate and cover with a tea towel while cooking the remaining batter.

Spread each warm crepe with almond mascarpone and fold into quarters. Serve the crepes topped with the strawberries, kiwi fruit, raspberries and blueberries.

NOTE: The crepes can be made ahead of time. Place a piece of baking paper between each crepe, wrap the whole stack in foil, then plastic wrap and refrigerate or freeze.

Rhubarb Crumble

🔺 SERVES 4–6
🔺 PREPARATION TIME: 15 MINUTES
🔺 COOKING TIME: 25 MINUTES

1 kg (2 lb 4 oz) rhubarb
170 g (6 oz/³⁄₄ cup) caster (superfine)
    sugar
100 g (3¹⁄₂ oz) unsalted butter
90 g (3¹⁄₄ oz/³⁄₄ cup) plain (all-purpose)
    flour
75 g (2³⁄₄ oz/¹⁄₃ cup) raw (demerara)
    sugar
10 amaretti biscuits (cookies), crushed

CRUNCHY MAPLE CREAM
200 ml (7 fl oz) thick (double/heavy)
    cream
2 tablespoons pure maple syrup or golden
    syrup
3 amaretti biscuits (cookies), crushed

Preheat the oven to 200°C (400°F/Gas 6). Trim the rhubarb, cut into short lengths and put in a saucepan with the sugar. Stir over low heat until the sugar has dissolved, then cover and simmer for 8–10 minutes, or until the rhubarb is soft but still chunky. Spoon into a deep 1.5 litre (52 fl oz/6 cup) ovenproof dish.

Rub the butter into the flour until the mixture resembles fine breadcrumbs, then stir in the demerara sugar and biscuits.

Sprinkle the crumble over the stewed rhubarb and bake for 15 minutes, or until the topping is golden brown.

To make the crunchy maple cream, place the cream in a bowl, carefully swirl the maple syrup through, then the crushed biscuits. Do not overmix – there should be rich veins of the crunchy syrup through the cream. Serve with the crumble.

Sicilian Rice Fritters

🔥 MAKES 8
🔥 PREPARATION TIME: 20 MINUTES +
🔥 COOKING TIME: 25 MINUTES

110 g (3¾ oz/½ cup) risotto rice
330 ml (11¼ fl oz/1⅓ cups) milk
10 g (¼ oz) unsalted butter
1 tablespoon caster (superfine) sugar
1 vanilla bean, scraped
1 teaspoon dried yeast
2 tablespoons cedro, finely chopped
2 teaspoons grated lemon zest
vegetable oil, for deep-frying
plain (all-purpose) flour, for rolling
2 tablespoons fragrant honey

Combine the rice, milk, butter, sugar, vanilla bean and scraped seeds and a pinch of salt in a heavy-based saucepan. Bring to the boil over medium heat, then reduce the heat to very low. Cover and cook for 15–18 minutes, or until most of the liquid has been absorbed. Remove from the heat, cover and set aside.

Dissolve the yeast in 2 tablespoons tepid water and allow to stand for 5 minutes, or until frothy. If your yeast doesn't foam, it is dead and you will have to start again.

Discard the vanilla bean from the rice mixture. Add the yeast, cedro and lemon zest to the rice. Mix well, cover and allow to stand for 1 hour.

Fill a deep-fryer or heavy-based saucepan one-third full of oil and heat to 180°C (350°F), or until a spoonful of the batter dropped into the oil browns in 15 seconds.

Shape the rice into croquettes about 2.5 x 8 cm (1 x 3¼ inches) and roll them in flour. Deep-fry in batches for 5–6 minutes, or until golden brown on all sides. Remove with a slotted spoon and drain on crumpled paper towel. Drizzle with honey and serve.

NOTES: Cedro, also known as citron, is a citrus fruit with a very thick, knobbly skin. The skin is used to make candied peel.

White Chocolate and Raspberry Ripple Rice Pudding

🔺 SERVES 4
🔺 PREPARATION TIME: 10 MINUTES
🔺 COOKING TIME: 30 MINUTES

120 g (4¼ oz/1 cup) raspberries
2 tablespoons icing (confectioners') sugar
2 tablespoons raspberry liqueur, such as Framboise
30 g (1 oz) unsalted butter
125 g (4½ oz/scant ⅔ cup) risotto rice
1 vanilla bean, split
800 ml (28 fl oz) milk
50 g (1¾ oz/¼ cup) caster (superfine) sugar
1 teaspoon natural vanilla extract
100 g (3½ oz/⅔ cup) chopped white chocolate

Using a hand blender, purée the raspberries, icing sugar and liqueur.

Melt the butter in a large non-stick saucepan. Add the rice and vanilla bean and stir until the rice is coated in butter. In a separate saucepan, heat the milk, caster sugar and vanilla to just below boiling. Ladle a spoonful of the milk mixture into the rice and stir constantly until the liquid has been absorbed. Repeat until all the milk mixture has been added and the rice is tender. Remove the vanilla bean (it can be dried and later re-used).

Add the white chocolate and stir until melted. Set aside for 5 minutes, then spoon the rice pudding into bowls. Swirl the raspberry purée through the rice to create a ripple effect.

Sweet Couscous

80 g (2³/₄ oz) combined pistachio nuts,
    pine nuts and blanched almonds
45 g (1¹/₂ oz/¹/₄ cup) dried apricots
90 g (3¹/₄ oz/¹/₂ cup) pitted dried dates
250 g (9 oz) instant couscous
55 g (2 oz/¹/₄ cup) caster (superfine)
    sugar
250 ml (9 fl oz/1 cup) boiling water
90 g (3¹/₄ oz) unsalted butter, softened

TO SERVE
2 tablespoons caster (superfine) sugar
¹/₂ teaspoon ground cinnamon
375 ml (13 fl oz/1¹/₂ cups) hot milk

Preheat the oven to 160°C (315°F/Gas 2–3). Spread the nuts on a baking tray and bake for 5 minutes, until light golden. Allow to cool, then roughly chop and place in a bowl. Slice the apricots into matchstick-sized pieces and quarter the dates lengthways. Add to the bowl and toss to combine.

Put the couscous and sugar in a large bowl and cover with the boiling water. Stir well, then add the butter and a pinch of salt. Stir until the butter melts. Cover with a tea towel and set aside for 10 minutes. Fluff with a fork, then toss half the fruit and nut mixture through.

To serve, pile the warm couscous in the centre of a platter. Arrange the remaining fruit and nut mixture around the base. Combine the sugar and cinnamon in a small bowl and serve separately for sprinkling. Pass around the hot milk for guests to help themselves.

Banana Fritters in Coconut Batter

🔺 SERVES 6

🔺 PREPARATION TIME: 15 MINUTES +

🔺 COOKING TIME: 20 MINUTES

100 g (3½ oz) glutinous rice flour
100 g (3½ oz) freshly grated coconut
    or 60 g (2¼ oz/⅔ cup)
    desiccated coconut
55 g (2 oz/¼ cup) sugar
1 tablespoon white sesame seeds
60 ml (2 fl oz/¼ cup) coconut milk
6 sugar bananas
oil, for deep-frying
vanilla ice cream, to serve
sesame seeds, toasted, extra, to garnish

Combine the flour, coconut, sugar, sesame seeds, coconut milk and 60 ml (2 fl oz/¼ cup) water in a large bowl. Whisk to a smooth batter, adding more water if the batter is too thick. Set aside to rest for 1 hour.

Peel the bananas and cut in half lengthways (cut each portion in half again crossways if the bananas are large).

Fill a wok or large heavy-based saucepan one-third full of oil and heat to 180°C (350°F), or until a cube of bread dropped into the oil browns in 15 seconds. Dip each piece of banana into the batter then drop gently into the hot oil. Cook in batches for 4–6 minutes, or until golden brown all over. Remove with a slotted spoon and drain on crumpled paper towel. Serve hot with vanilla ice cream and a sprinkling of extra toasted sesame seeds.

Stuffed Figs

🌲 MAKES 18
🌲 PREPARATION TIME: 30 MINUTES +
🌲 COOKING TIME: 30 MINUTES

175 g (6 oz/¹/₂ cup) honey
125 ml (4 fl oz/¹/₂ cup) sweet dark sherry
¹/₄ teaspoon ground cinnamon
18 large dried figs
18 whole blanched almonds
100 g (3¹/₂ oz) dark chocolate,
    cut into shards
thick (double/heavy) cream, to serve

Put the honey, sherry, cinnamon, figs and 375 ml (13 fl oz/1¹/₂ cups) water in a large saucepan over high heat. Bring to the boil, then reduce the heat and simmer for 10 minutes. Remove the pan from the heat and set aside for 3 hours. Remove the figs with a slotted spoon, reserving the liquid. Preheat the oven to 180°C (350°F/Gas 4).

Return the pan of liquid to the heat and boil for 5 minutes, or until syrupy, then set aside.

Cut the stems from the figs, then cut a slit in the top of each fig. Push an almond and a few shards of chocolate into each slit. Put the figs in a lightly buttered ovenproof dish and bake for 15 minutes, or until the chocolate has melted. Serve with a little of the syrup and some cream.

Sago Plum Pudding with Rum Butter

🔺 SERVES 6–8

🔺 PREPARATION TIME: 35 MINUTES +

🔺 COOKING TIME: 4 HOURS

65 g (2¼ oz/⅓ cup) sago
250 ml (9 fl oz/1 cup) milk
1 teaspoon bicarbonate of soda
    (baking soda)
140 g (5 oz/¾ cup) dark brown sugar
160 g (5¾ oz/2 cups) fresh white
    breadcrumbs
80 g (2¾ oz/½ cup) sultanas
    (golden raisins)
75 g (2½ oz/½ cup) currants
80 g (2¾ oz/½ cup) dried dates, chopped
2 eggs, lightly beaten
60 g (2¼ oz) unsalted butter, melted
    and cooled
raspberries, to decorate
blueberries, to decorate
icing (confectioners') sugar, to decorate

RUM BUTTER
125 g (4½ oz) butter, softened
140 g (5 oz/¾ cup) dark brown sugar
80 ml (2½ fl oz/⅓ cup) rum

Combine the sago and milk in a bowl, cover and refrigerate overnight.

Lightly grease a 1.5 litre (52 fl oz/6 cup) pudding basin (mould) with butter and line the base with baking paper. Place the empty basin in a large saucepan on a trivet or upturned saucer and pour in enough cold water to come halfway up the side of the basin. Remove the basin and put the water on to boil.

Transfer the soaked sago and milk to a large bowl and stir in the bicarbonate of soda until dissolved. Stir in the sugar, breadcrumbs, dried fruit, beaten eggs and melted butter and mix well. Spoon into the basin and smooth the surface with wet hands.

Cover the basin with the lid and make a string handle. Gently lower the basin into the boiling water, reduce to a fast simmer and cover the saucepan with a tight-fitting lid. Cook for 3½–4 hours, or until a skewer inserted into the centre of the pudding comes out clean. Check the water level every hour and top up with boiling water as necessary.

Carefully remove the pudding basin from the saucepan, remove the coverings and leave for 5 minutes before turning out the pudding onto a large serving plate. Loosen the edges with a palette knife, if necessary. Serve decorated with raspberries and blueberries and lightly dusted with icing sugar. Serve hot with cold rum butter.

To make the rum butter, beat the butter and sugar with electric beaters for about 3–4 minutes, or until light and creamy. Gradually beat in the rum, 1 tablespoon at a time. You can add more rum, to taste. Transfer to a serving dish, cover and refrigerate until required.

NOTE: Sago is the starch extracted from the sago palm. It is dried and formed into balls by pushing through a sieve. It is often called pearl sago and is available from supermarkets or health food stores. It is white when uncooked but goes transparent when cooked.

Israeli Doughnuts

🌿 MAKES 14

🌿 PREPARATION TIME: 40 MINUTES +

🌿 COOKING TIME: 25 MINUTES

185 ml (6 fl oz/¾ cup) lukewarm milk

1 tablespoon dried yeast

2 tablespoons caster (superfine) sugar

310 g (11 oz/2½ cups) plain
    (all-purpose) flour

2 teaspoons ground cinnamon

1 teaspoon finely grated lemon zest

2 eggs, separated

40 g (1½ oz) unsalted butter, softened

105 g (3¾ oz/⅓ cup) plum, strawberry
    or apricot jam

oil, for deep-frying

caster (superfine) sugar, extra, for rolling

Put the milk in a small bowl, add the yeast and 1 tablespoon of the sugar. Leave in a warm, draught-free place for 10 minutes, or until bubbles appear on the surface. The mixture should be frothy and slightly increased in volume. If your yeast doesn't foam, it is dead, so you will have to discard it and start again.

Sift the flour into a large bowl and add the cinnamon, lemon zest, egg yolks, yeast mixture, remaining sugar, and a pinch of salt. Mix well, then place the dough on a lightly floured work surface and knead for 5 minutes. Work in the butter, a little at a time, continually kneading until the dough becomes elastic. This should take about 10 minutes. Place in a large bowl and cover with a clean, damp tea towel (dish towel). Leave to rise overnight in the refrigerator.

Place the dough on a lightly floured work surface and roll out to 3 mm (⅛ inch) thick. Using a 6 cm (2½ inch) cutter, cut 28 rounds from the dough. Place 14 of the rounds on a lightly floured tray and carefully place ¾ teaspoon of the jam into the centre of each. Lightly beat the egg whites, then brush a little around the outside edges of the rounds, being careful not to touch the jam at all. Top with the remaining 14 rounds and press down firmly around the edges to seal. Cover with a clean tea towel and leave to rise for 30 minutes. Make sure the dough has not separated at the edges. Press any open edges firmly together.

Fill a deep-fryer or large heavy-based saucepan one-third full of oil and heat to 170°C (325°F), or until a cube of bread dropped into the oil browns in 20 seconds. Cook the doughnuts in batches for 1½ minutes on both sides, or until golden. Drain on crumpled paper towel and roll in the extra caster sugar. Serve immediately.

Steamed Chocolate and Prune Puddings with Cognac Cream

🔺 SERVES 8
🔺 PREPARATION TIME: 30 MINUTES
🔺 COOKING TIME: 50 MINUTES

melted butter, to grease
125 g (4½ oz) unsalted butter, softened
125 g (4½ oz/⅔ cup) soft brown sugar
3 eggs, at room temperature
125 g (4½ oz/1 cup) self-raising flour
40 g (1½ oz/⅓ cup) unsweetened cocoa
    powder
60 ml (2 fl oz/¼ cup) milk
125 g (4½ oz) dark couverture chocolate
    (54% cocoa), finely chopped
125 g (4½ oz) pitted prunes, chopped
icing (confectioners') sugar, to dust

COGNAC CREAM
300 ml (10½ fl oz) cream
2 tablespoons icing (confectioners') sugar,
    sifted
2 tablespoons Cognac or brandy

Preheat the oven to 180°C (350°F/Gas 4). Brush eight 185 ml (6 fl oz/¾ cup) ramekins with the melted butter. Line the bases with rounds of baking paper.

Beat the butter and sugar in a mixing bowl with electric beaters until pale and creamy. Add the eggs one at a time, beating well after each addition. Sift together the flour and cocoa powder over the butter mixture, and fold together until just combined. Fold in the milk, then the chocolate and prunes until evenly combined.

Spoon the mixture into the ramekins and smooth the surface with the back of a spoon. Cover each pudding with a piece of buttered foil, folding the edges of the foil tightly around the rims of the ramekins.

Place the ramekins in an ovenproof dish. Add enough boiling water to the ovenproof dish to come halfway up the sides of the ramekins. Bake for 45–50 minutes, or until the puddings are cooked when tested with a skewer.

To make the cognac cream, combine the cream, icing sugar and Cognac in a small bowl and stir until evenly combined. Cover and place in the refrigerator.

Stand the puddings for 5 minutes before turning onto serving plates. Dust with icing sugar and serve with a dollop of cognac cream on the side.

NOTE: Puddings will keep for up to 2 days in the refrigerator in the ramekins, covered with plastic wrap (the foil removed). Turn onto serving plates before reheating in the microwave.

Sweet Cheese in Lemon Pasta

🌢 SERVES 4–6
🌢 PREPARATION TIME: 1 HOUR +
🌢 COOKING TIME: 25 MINUTES

PASTA
250 g (9 oz/2 cups) plain
    (all-purpose) flour
1/2 teaspoon salt
1 teaspoon caster (superfine) sugar
grated zest of 2 lemons
2 tablespoons lemon juice
2 eggs, lightly beaten

FILLING
1 tablespoon currants
1 tablespoon brandy
600 g (1 lb 5 oz) ricotta cheese
40 g (1 1/2 oz/1/3 cup) icing
    (confectioners') sugar
3/4 teaspoon grated lemon zest
3/4 teaspoon natural vanilla extract
30 g (1 oz/1/3 cup) flaked almonds, toasted

beaten egg, for glazing
vegetable oil, for frying
250 ml (9 fl oz/1 cup) cream, flavoured
    with brandy, to taste
icing (confectioners') sugar, to sprinkle
mint leaves, to garnish
thin strips of lemon zest, to garnish,
    (optional)

To make the pasta, pile the combined flour, salt, sugar and lemon zest on a work surface and make a well in the centre. Add 1–2 tablespoons water, the lemon juice and egg and gradually blend them into the flour, using a fork. When a loosely combined dough forms, use your hands and begin kneading. Incorporate a little extra flour if the dough feels moist. Knead for 5–8 minutes, or until smooth and elastic. Cover with plastic wrap and set aside for 15 minutes.

Soak the currants in the brandy in a bowl. In a larger bowl, combine the ricotta cheese, icing sugar, lemon zest and vanilla. Set aside.

Divide the dough into eight equal portions. Roll each out to a thin sheet about 18 cm (7 inch) square. Cover each as it is completed with plastic wrap.

Trim each pasta sheet into a neat square. Working with a few at a time, brush around the edges with beaten egg. Add the currants and toasted almonds to the ricotta filling, then put one-eighth of the filling in the middle of each square of dough. Fold the edges over to completely enclose the filling. Press the edges down to seal.

Heat the oil in a pan to 1–2 cm (about 1/2 inch) depth. Drop a piece of scrap pasta in to check that it turns golden without burning. Fry the parcels, two or three at a time, until golden. Remove with a slotted spoon, drain on paper towel and keep warm. Serve with brandy cream. Sprinkle with icing sugar and garnish with mint leaves and lemon zest, if desired.

Peach Charlottes with Melba Sauce

🔺 SERVES 4
🔺 PREPARATION TIME: 30 MINUTES +
🔺 COOKING TIME: 40 MINUTES

220 g (7¾ oz/1 cup) sugar
6 peaches, unpeeled
80 ml (2½ fl oz/⅓ cup) peach liqueur
2 loaves brioche
100 g (3½ oz) butter, melted
160 g (5½ oz/½ cup) apricot jam,
    warmed and sieved
raspberries, extra, to serve

MELBA SAUCE
300 g (10½ oz) fresh or thawed frozen
    raspberries
2 tablespoons icing (confectioners') sugar

Preheat the oven to 180°C (350°F/Gas 4). Brush four 250 ml (9 fl oz/1 cup) ovenproof ramekins or dariole moulds with melted butter.

Put the sugar and 1 litre (35 fl oz/4 cups) water in a large heavy-based saucepan. Stir over medium heat until the sugar completely dissolves. Bring to the boil, then reduce the heat slightly and add the whole peaches. Simmer, covered, for 20 minutes. Drain and cool. Peel the skins and slice the flesh thickly. Place the peach slices in a bowl, sprinkle with the liqueur and set aside for 20 minutes.

Cut the brioche into 1 cm (½ inch) thick slices and remove the crusts. With a scone-cutter, cut out rounds to fit the tops and bases of each ramekin. Cut the remaining slices into 2 cm (¾ inch) wide strips and trim to fit the height of the ramekins. Dip the first round into melted butter and place in the base of the ramekin. Dip the brioche strips into the melted butter and press around the side of the ramekin, overlapping slightly. Line all the ramekins with the brioche in this manner.

Fill the lined ramekins evenly with peach slices and top each with the last round of brioche dipped in melted butter. Press to seal. Put the ramekins on a baking tray and bake for 20 minutes.

Meanwhile, make the Melba sauce. Put the berries in a food processor and add the icing sugar (you may need a little more, depending on the sweetness of the berries). Process until smooth, then push the berries through a fine sieve.

Turn the peach charlottes out onto serving plates, brush with the warmed jam and pour some Melba sauce alongside. Serve with extra berries if desired.

NOTE: The peaches can be cooked, the ramekins lined with brioche and the Melba sauce made up to 6 hours ahead. Refrigerate the charlottes, then fill and bake them close to serving time.

Chocolate Puddings with Malt Cream

🔺 SERVES 6

🔺 PREPARATION TIME: 20 MINUTES

🔺 COOKING TIME: 15 MINUTES

200 g (7 oz) dark couverture chocolate
    (54% cocoa), chopped
100 g (3¹/₂ oz) unsalted butter, cubed
2 eggs, at room temperature
2 egg yolks, at room temperature
55 g (2 oz/¹/₄ cup) caster (superfine)
    sugar
2 tablespoons plain (all-purpose) flour,
    sifted
unsweetened cocoa powder, to dust

MALT CREAM
200 ml (7 fl oz) whipping cream
45 g (1¹/₂ oz/¹/₃ cup) malted milk powder
1 tablespoon icing (confectioners') sugar,
    sifted

Preheat the oven to 180°C (350°F/Gas 4). Brush six 185 ml (6 fl oz/³/₄ cup) ramekins with melted butter. Place them on a baking tray.

Combine the chocolate and butter in a small saucepan over low heat. Stir frequently until the mixture is smooth. Remove from the heat.

Beat the whole eggs, egg yolks and sugar in a bowl with electric beaters until thick and pale. Add the chocolate mixture and flour and fold in until evenly combined.

Spoon the chocolate mixture evenly into the ramekins. Bake for 12 minutes, or until the puddings have risen almost to the top of the ramekins (they will still look slightly underdone).

To make the malt cream, place the cream, malted milk powder and icing sugar in a bowl. Use a balloon whisk to whisk the mixture until soft peaks form. Cover and place in the refrigerator until ready to serve.

Turn the puddings onto serving plates. Sprinkle with cocoa powder and serve with a dollop of the malt cream on the side.

Pecan Brownies

🔺 MAKES 16
🔺 PREPARATION TIME: 20 MINUTES
🔺 COOKING TIME: 35 MINUTES

125 g (4½ oz) dark chocolate, chopped
90 g (3¼ oz) unsalted butter, softened
230 g (8 oz/1 cup) caster (superfine)
    sugar
1 teaspoon natural vanilla extract
2 eggs
85 g (3 oz/⅔ cup) plain (all-purpose)
    flour
30 g (1 oz/¼ cup) unsweetened cocoa
    powder
½ teaspoon baking powder
125 g (4½ oz/1 cup) roughly chopped
    pecans

Preheat the oven to 180°C (350°F/Gas 4). Grease a 17 cm (6¾ inch) square cake tin and line the base with baking paper, leaving the paper hanging over two opposite sides.

Put the chocolate in a heatproof bowl. Half-fill a saucepan with water and bring to the boil, then remove the pan from the heat. Sit the bowl over the pan, making sure the base of the bowl doesn't touch the water. Stir occasionally until the chocolate has melted. Cool slightly.

Beat the butter, sugar and vanilla in a bowl with electric beaters until the mixture is thick and creamy. Add the eggs one at a time, beating well after each addition. Stir in the melted chocolate.

Sift the flour, cocoa powder and baking powder into a bowl, then use a metal spoon to fold the flour mixture into the chocolate. Fold in the pecans. Spoon the mixture into the tin and smooth out the surface.

Bake for 30–35 minutes, or until firm and the cake comes away from the sides of the tin. Cool in the tin, then remove and cut into squares.

Chocolate Beetroot Cakes

⚜ MAKES 8

⚜ PREPARATION TIME: 30 MINUTES

⚜ COOKING TIME: 20 MINUTES

125 g (4½ oz/1 cup) plain (all-purpose)
    flour
40 g (1½ oz/⅓ cup) unsweetened cocoa
    powder
1½ teaspoons bicarbonate of soda
    (baking soda)
½ teaspoon baking powder
1 teaspoon mixed spice (optional)
230 g (8½ oz/1 cup) firmly packed soft
    brown sugar
75 g (2¾ oz/¾ cup) walnut halves,
    chopped
170 ml (5½ fl oz/⅔ cup) canola or
    vegetable oil
2 eggs, at room temperature
225 g (8 oz/1½ cups) firmly packed
    finely grated raw beetroot

CHOCOLATE ICING (FROSTING)
160 g (5½ oz/1¼ cups) icing
    (confectioners') sugar
30 g (1 oz/¼ cup) unsweetened cocoa
    powder
60 ml (2 fl oz/¼ cup) boiling water

Preheat the oven to 180°C (350°F/Gas 4). Grease eight 250 ml (9 fl oz/1 cup) fluted ring tins with oil. Place them on a large baking tray

In a large bowl, sift the flour, cocoa powder, bicarbonate of soda, baking powder and mixed spice, if using. Stir in the brown sugar and walnuts. Make a well in the centre of the bowl.

Whisk the oil and eggs in a bowl until well combined. Add the beetroot and stir to combine. Add to the flour mixture and fold together with a large metal spoon until just combined. Spoon the mixture into the tins and smooth out the surfaces.

Bake for 20 minutes, or until cooked when tested with a skewer. Leave the cakes in the tins for 5 minutes before turning onto a wire rack to cool.

To make the chocolate icing, sift the icing sugar and cocoa powder into a bowl. Add the boiling water and mix until smooth. Place the cakes on the wire rack over a tray. Drizzle the icing over the cakes. Set aside for 30 minutes, or until the icing has set. Serve the cakes on their own or with thick cream or vanilla ice cream.

NOTE: The cakes, either iced or un-iced, will keep in an airtight container at room temperature for up to 3 days. To freeze, wrap individual un-iced cakes in plastic wrap. Place in a sealed freezer bag or in an airtight container and freeze for up to 1 month. Thaw at room temperature.

Chocolate French Toast

🌿 SERVES 2

🌿 PREPARATION TIME: 15 MINUTES

🌿 COOKING TIME: 10 MINUTES

60 g (2¼ oz) dark couverture chocolate
    (54% cocoa), chopped
4 x 1.5 cm (⅝ inch) thick slices day-old
    brioche
1 egg, at room temperature
1½ tablespoons cream
1½ tablespoons milk
1 tablespoon caster (superfine) sugar
½ teaspoon natural vanilla extract
¼ teaspoon ground cinnamon
20 g (¾ oz) butter
icing (confectioners') sugar, to dust

Put the chocolate in a heatproof bowl. Half-fill a saucepan with water and bring to the boil, then remove the pan from the heat. Sit the bowl over the pan, making sure the base of the bowl doesn't touch the water. Stir until the chocolate just melts and the mixture is smooth. Remove the bowl from the pan.

Spread the chocolate mixture over 2 slices of brioche and sandwich together with the remaining slices.

Whisk the egg, cream, milk, sugar, vanilla and cinnamon in a shallow bowl. Soak the sandwiches in the egg mixture, allowing about 30 seconds for each side to soak up the bread.

Melt the butter in a large non-stick frying pan over medium heat. When the butter is sizzling, remove the sandwiches, allowing any excess egg mixture to drain off, and place in the pan. Cook for 2 minutes each side, or until well browned. Cut the sandwiches in half and dust with icing sugar before serving.

NOTE: You can also use 4 slices of hand-cut cob or cottage loaf instead of the brioche if you wish.

Kheer Rice Pudding

⚶ SERVES 4
⚶ PREPARATION TIME: 15 MINUTES +
⚶ COOKING TIME: 1 HOUR 50 MINUTES

65 g (2½ oz/⅓ cup) basmati rice
1.5 litres (52 fl oz/6 cups) milk
6 cardamom pods, lightly crushed
115 g (4 oz/½ cup) caster (superfine)
   sugar
40 g (1½ oz/¼ cup) chopped raisins
30 g (1 oz/¼ cup) slivered almonds
pinch of saffron threads
1 tablespoon rosewater (optional)
ground cinnamon (optional)

Soak the rice in water for 30 minutes, then drain.

Pour the milk into a saucepan, add the cardamom pods and bring to the boil. Add the rice, reduce the heat and simmer for 1 hour, stirring often, until the rice is cooked. Add the sugar, raisins and slivered almonds, bring to a low boil and cook for 50 minutes, or until the mixture is the consistency of porridge. Stir frequently to avoid it sticking to the base of the pan. Remove the cardamom pods.

Mix the saffron threads with a little water and add just enough to the mixture to give the pudding a pale yellow colour. Allow to cool, then stir in the rosewater, if using. Serve warm or cold with a sprinkling of cinnamon on top, if desired.

NOTE: Kheer is a rich and creamy dessert, with the cardamom and almonds giving it a distinctive texture and flavour. It is usually served at banquets, weddings and religious ceremonies in India, where it is known as the 'Queen of desserts' or 'Queen of creams'.

Banana and Coconut Pancakes

SERVES 4–6

PREPARATION TIME: 10 MINUTES

COOKING TIME: 30 MINUTES

1 tablespoon shredded coconut
40 g (1½ oz/⅓ cup) plain (all-purpose)
    flour
2 tablespoons rice flour
55 g (2 oz/¼ cup) caster (superfine)
    sugar
25 g (1 oz/¼ cup) desiccated coconut
250 ml (9 fl oz/1 cup) coconut milk
1 egg, lightly beaten
butter, for frying
60 g (2¼ oz) butter, extra
4 large bananas, cut diagonally into
    thick slices
60 g (2¼ oz/⅓ cup) soft brown sugar
80 ml (2½ fl oz/⅓ cup) lime juice
grated lime zest, to serve

Spread the shredded coconut on a baking tray and toast it in a 150°C (300°F/Gas 2) oven for 10 minutes, or until it is dark golden, shaking the tray occasionally. Remove from the tray and set aside. Sift the flours into a bowl. Add the sugar and desiccated coconut and mix. Make a well in the centre, pour in the combined coconut milk and egg, and beat until smooth.

Melt a little butter in a non-stick frying pan. Pour 60 ml (2 fl oz/¼ cup) of the pancake mixture into the pan and cook over medium heat until the underside is golden. Turn the pancake over and cook the other side. Transfer to a plate and cover with a tea towel (dish towel) to keep warm. Repeat with the remaining pancake batter, buttering the pan when necessary.

Heat the extra butter in the pan, add the banana, toss until coated, and cook over medium heat until the banana starts to soften and brown. Sprinkle with the brown sugar and shake the pan gently until the sugar has melted. Stir in the lime juice. Divide the banana among the pancakes and fold over to enclose. Sprinkle with the toasted coconut and lime zest.

The Ultimate Hot Chocolate

🔥 SERVES 2
🔥 PREPARATION TIME: 5 MINUTES
🔥 COOKING TIME: 10 MINUTES

60 g (2¼ oz) dark chocolate, roughly
    chopped
500 ml (17 fl oz/2 cups) hot milk
marshmallows, to serve

Put the chocolate in a small pan. Add 2 tablespoons water and stir over low heat until the chocolate has melted. Gradually pour in the hot milk, whisking until smooth and slightly frothy. Heat the chocolate milk without boiling.

Pour the hot chocolate into mugs and place one or two marshmallows on top.

Rice Pudding with Berries

🔥 MAKES 24
🔥 PREPARATION TIME: 10 MINUTES
🔥 COOKING TIME: 15 MINUTES

220 g (7¾ oz/1 cup) short-grain rice
125 g (4½ oz/½ cup) plain yoghurt
300 ml (10½ fl oz) cream
80 g (2¾ oz/⅓ cup) caster (superfine)
    sugar
1 teaspoon natural vanilla extract
250 g (9 oz) strawberries, hulled and
    halved
300 g (10½ oz) fresh or frozen
    blueberries
1 tablespoon caster (superfine) sugar,
    extra

Put the rice, ½ teaspoon salt and 625 ml (21½ fl oz/ 2½ cups) water in a saucepan and bring to the boil over high heat, stirring once. Reduce the heat and simmer, covered, for 20 minutes, or until the rice is very soft and tender but the mixture is still moist. Remove from the heat and leave for 5 minutes.

Put the yoghurt, cream, sugar and vanilla in a bowl and whisk together. Leave at room temperature, stirring occasionally to dissolve the sugar.

Toss the strawberries, blueberries and extra sugar together in a bowl. Cover and refrigerate until ready to serve.

Stir the hot rice into the cream mixture. Add more milk or cream if the mixture is too thick. Serve topped with the strawberries and blueberries.

The Ultimate Hot Chocolate

Chocolate Banana Cake

🔺 SERVES 6–8
🔺 PREPARATION TIME: 15 MINUTES
🔺 COOKING TIME: 55 MINUTES

3 ripe bananas, mashed
170 g (6 oz/³/4 cup) caster (superfine)
    sugar
185 g (6¹/2 oz/1¹/2 cups) self-raising flour
2 eggs, lightly beaten
60 ml (2 fl oz/¹/4 cup) light olive oil
60 ml (2 fl oz/¹/4 cup) milk
100 g (3¹/2 oz) dark chocolate, grated
90 g (3¹/4 oz/³/4 cup) chopped walnuts

Preheat the oven to 180°C (350°F/Gas 4). Lightly grease a 20 x 10 cm (8 x 4 inch) loaf (bar) tin and line the base with baking paper.

Mix the mashed banana and sugar in a large bowl until just combined. Add the sifted flour, eggs, oil and milk. Stir the mixture gently for 30 seconds with a wooden spoon. Fold in the chocolate and walnuts.

Pour the mixture into the tin and bake for 55 minutes, or until a skewer comes out clean when inserted into the centre of the cake. Leave to cool in the tin for 5 minutes before turning onto a wire rack. If desired, serve warm with cream.

NOTE: In warm weather, chocolate can be grated more easily if it is left to harden in the freezer for a few minutes before grating.

Chocolate Rum Fondue

🔥 SERVES 6
🔥 PREPARATION TIME: 10 MINUTES
🔥 COOKING TIME: 5 MINUTES

250 g (9 oz) dark chocolate, chopped
125 ml (4 fl oz/$\frac{1}{2}$ cup) cream
1–2 tablespoons rum

1 mandarin, tangerine or small orange,
    peeled and divided into segments
2 fresh figs, quartered lengthways
250 g (9 oz/1$\frac{2}{3}$ cups) strawberries
250 g (9 oz/2$\frac{3}{4}$ cups) white marshmallows

Put the chocolate and cream in a heatproof bowl. Half-fill a saucepan with water and bring to the boil, then remove the pan from the heat. Sit the bowl over the pan, making sure the base of the bowl doesn't touch the water. Stir until the chocolate mixture is smooth. Remove from the heat and stir in the rum to taste. While still warm, pour the chocolate mixture into the fondue pot.

Arrange the fruit and marshmallows on a serving platter and serve with the chocolate fondue.

NOTE: Use a selection of fruit in season. If the fruit needs to be cut, avoid using fruit with a moist surface.

Baked Chocolate Custards

30 g (1 oz) unsalted butter, melted

55 g (2 oz/¼ cup) caster (superfine) sugar, for dusting

300 ml (10½ fl oz) cream

200 ml (7 fl oz) milk

200 g (7 oz) dark chocolate, roughly chopped

grated zest from 1 orange

6 eggs

115 g (4 oz/½ cup) caster (superfine) sugar, extra

raspberries, to serve

icing (confectioners') sugar, for dusting

Preheat the oven to 160°C (315°F/Gas 2–3). Grease ten 125 ml (4 fl oz/½ cup) ramekins with butter and dust the inside of each with caster sugar.

Put the cream and milk in a saucepan over low heat and bring almost to the boil. Add the chocolate and stir over low heat until the chocolate has melted and is well combined. Stir in the orange zest.

Whisk the eggs and sugar in a large bowl for 5 minutes, or until pale and thick. Whisk a little of the hot chocolate cream into the eggs, then pour the egg mixture onto the remaining chocolate cream, whisking continuously.

Divide the mixture among the ramekins. Place the ramekins in an ovenproof dish. Add enough boiling water to the dish to come halfway up the sides of the ramekins. Cover the tin with foil and bake for 30–35 minutes, or until the custards are set.

Remove the ramekins from the water bath and set aside to cool completely. Turn the custards out onto serving plates. Top with the raspberries and dust with icing sugar before serving.

White Chocolate and Almond Cupcakes

🔺 SERVES 12
🔺 PREPARATION TIME: 30 MINUTES
🔺 COOKING TIME: 25 MINUTES

125 g (4½ oz) white chocolate, chopped
80 g (2¾ oz) unsalted butter, cubed
100 ml (3½ fl oz) milk
115 g (4 oz/½ cup) caster (superfine)
   sugar
1 egg, at room temperature
90 g (3¼ oz/¾ cup) self-raising flour,
   sifted
55 g (2 oz/½ cup) ground almonds
240 g (8½ oz) raspberries, to decorate
icing (confectioners') sugar, to dust

WHITE CHOCOLATE GANACHE
400 g (14 oz) white chocolate, finely
   chopped
170 ml (5½ fl oz/⅔ cup) pouring cream

Preheat the oven to 190°C (375°F/Gas 5). Line a 12-hole standard muffin tin with paper cases.

Combine the chocolate, butter and milk in a small saucepan. Stir over low heat until the chocolate and butter have melted and the mixture is smooth. Remove from the heat and transfer to a large bowl. Set aside until lukewarm.

Whisk the sugar and egg into the chocolate mixture until well combined. Combine the flour and ground almonds, add to the chocolate mixture and stir until just combined.

Spoon the mixture evenly into the paper cases. Bake for 18 minutes, or until the cakes are just cooked when tested with a skewer. Leave the cakes to cool in the tin for 5 minutes before turning out onto a wire rack.

To make the white chocolate ganache, put the chocolate in a heatproof bowl. Heat the cream in a small pan until almost simmering. Add the cream to the chocolate and set aside for 1 minute, then stir until the mixture is smooth. Place in the refrigerator, and take out occasionally to stir until the mixture becomes a thick, spreadable consistency.

Decorate each cake with ganache, top with a raspberry and dust with icing sugar.

Sacher Torte

🌲 MAKES 1
🌲 PREPARATION TIME: 40 MINUTES
🌲 COOKING TIME: 55 MINUTES

125 g (4 oz/1 cup) plain (all-purpose) flour

30 g (1 oz/¼ cup) unsweetened cocoa powder

230 g (8 oz/1 cup) caster (superfine) sugar

100 g (3½ oz) unsalted butter

80 g (2¾ oz/¼ cup) strawberry jam

4 eggs, separated

GANACHE TOPPING

170 ml (5½ fl oz/⅔ cup) cream

90 g (3 oz/⅓ cup) caster (superfine) sugar

200 g (7 oz) dark chocolate, chopped

Preheat the oven to 180°C (350°F/Gas 4). Lightly grease a 20 cm (8 inch) round cake tin and line the base with baking paper.

Sift the flour and cocoa powder into a large bowl and make a well. Combine the sugar, butter and half the jam in a small saucepan. Stir over low heat until the butter is melted and the sugar has dissolved, then add the butter mixture to the flour. Lightly beat the egg yolks and stir into the mixture until just combined.

Beat the egg whites in a small bowl with electric beaters until soft peaks form. Stir a third of the egg white into the cake mixture, then fold in the rest in two batches.

Pour the mixture into the prepared tin and smooth out the surface. Bake for 40–45 minutes, or until a skewer comes out clean when inserted into the cake. Leave the cake to cool in the tin for 15 minutes before turning out onto a wire rack.

To make the ganache topping, combine the cream, sugar and chocolate in a small saucepan over low heat, stirring until the mixture has melted and is smooth.

Trim the top of the cake so that it is flat, then turn it upside down on a wire rack over a tray. Melt the remaining jam and brush it over the cake. Pour most of the ganache topping over the cake and tap the tray to flatten the surface. Place the remaining mixture in a piping (icing) bag and pipe 'Sacher' on the top of the cake.

Angel Food Cake with Chocolate Sauce

🌿 SERVES 8

🌿 PREPARATION TIME: 30 MINUTES

🌿 COOKING TIME: 45 MINUTES

125 g (4½ oz/1 cup) plain (all-purpose)
   flour
230 g (8 oz/1 cup) caster (superfine)
   sugar
10 egg whites, at room temperature
1 teaspoon cream of tartar
½ teaspoon natural vanilla extract

CHOCOLATE SAUCE
250 g (9 oz) dark chocolate, chopped
185 ml (6 fl oz/¾ cup) cream
50 g (1¾ oz) unsalted butter, chopped

Preheat the oven to 180°C (350°F/Gas 4). Have an ungreased angel cake tin ready. Sift the flour and half the sugar four times into a large bowl. Set aside.

Beat the egg whites, cream of tartar and ¼ teaspoon salt in another large bowl with electric beaters until soft peaks form. Gradually add the remaining sugar and beat until thick and glossy. Add the vanilla.

Sift half the flour and sugar mixture over the meringue and gently fold into the mixture with a metal spoon. Repeat with the remaining flour and sugar. Spoon into the cake tin and bake for 45 minutes, or until a skewer comes out clean when inserted into the centre of the cake. Gently loosen around the side of the cake with a spatula, then turn the cake out onto a wire rack to cool completely.

To make the chocolate sauce, put the chocolate, cream and butter in a saucepan. Stir over low heat until the chocolate has melted and the mixture is smooth. Drizzle over the cake and serve.

NOTE: Ensure that the tin is very clean and not greased or the cake will not rise and will slip down the side of the tin.

Rich Chocolate and Whisky Mud Cake with Sugared Violets

🌿 SERVES 16–20
🌿 PREPARATION TIME: 20 MINUTES
🌿 COOKING TIME: 1 HOUR 30 MINUTES

250 g (9 oz) butter, chopped
200 g (7 oz) dark chocolate, chopped
375 g (13 oz/1²/₃ cups) caster (superfine)
    sugar
125 ml (4 fl oz/¹/₂ cup) whisky
1 tablespoon instant coffee granules
185 g (6¹/₂ oz/1¹/₂ cups) plain
    (all-purpose) flour
60 g (2¹/₄ oz/¹/₂ cup) self-raising flour
40 g (1¹/₂ oz/¹/₃ cup) unsweetened cocoa
    powder
2 eggs, lightly beaten
3 tablespoons whisky, extra

CHOCOLATE GLAZE
80 ml (2¹/₂ fl oz/¹/₃ cup) cream
90 g (3¹/₄ oz) dark chocolate, chopped

sugared violets, to decorate
silver cachous, to decorate (optional)

Preheat the oven to 160°C (315°F/Gas 2–3). Grease a 20 cm (8 inch) square cake tin and line the base and sides with baking paper.

Put the butter, chocolate, sugar and whisky in a saucepan. Dissolve the coffee granules in 125 ml (4 fl oz/¹/₂ cup) hot water and add to the mixture. Stir over low heat until the granules are melted and the mixture is smooth.

Sift the flours and cocoa powder into a large bowl. Pour the butter mixture onto the flour mixture and whisk until just combined. Whisk in the eggs. Pour the mixture into the prepared tin.

Bake for 1 hour 15 minutes, or until a skewer comes out clean when inserted into the centre of the cake. Pour the extra whisky over the hot cooked cake. Leave in the tin for 20 minutes, then turn out onto a wire rack placed over a baking tray to cool completely.

To make the chocolate glaze, put the cream in a small saucepan and bring just to the boil. Remove from the heat. Add the chocolate, then stir until combined and smooth. Set aside to cool and thicken a little. Spread the glaze over the cake, allowing it to drizzle over the sides. Leave to set. Decorate with the sugared violets and silver cachousm if desired.

NOTE: To make the sugared violets, use a small, clean artist's paintbrush to coat 16 fresh unsprayed violets with a thin layer of lightly beaten egg white. Sprinkle evenly with caster sugar. Stand the violets on a wire rack and leave to dry. When dry, store them in an airtight container between layers of tissue. The violets are edible.

Chocolate Rum 'n' Raisin Cake

🌲 SERVES 8

🌲 PREPARATION TIME: 20 MINUTES +

🌲 COOKING TIME: 1 HOUR 15 MINUTES

2 tablespoons dark rum

40 g (1½ oz/⅓ cup) raisins, finely chopped

165 g (5¾ oz/1⅓ cups) self-raising flour

40 g (1½ oz/⅓ cup) plain (all-purpose) flour

40 g (1½ oz/⅓ cup) unsweetened cocoa powder

170 g (6 oz/¾ cup) caster (superfine) sugar

35 g (1¼ oz/¼ cup) raw (demerara) sugar

200 g (7 oz) unsalted butter

1 tablespoon golden syrup

100 g (3½ oz/⅔ cup) chopped dark chocolate

2 eggs, lightly beaten

unsweetened cocoa powder, to dust

icing (confectioners') sugar, to dust

whipped cream, to serve

Preheat the oven to 160°C (315°F/Gas 2–3). Grease a deep 20 cm (8 inch) round cake tin. Line the base and sides of the tin with baking paper.

Combine the rum, raisins and 60 ml (2 fl oz/¼ cup) of hot water in a small bowl and set aside. Sift the flours and cocoa powder into a large bowl and make a well in the centre.

Combine the caster sugar, raw sugar, butter, golden syrup and chocolate in a medium saucepan. Stir over low heat until the butter and chocolate have melted and all the sugar has dissolved. Remove from the heat. Stir in the rum and raisin mixture.

Using a metal spoon, stir the butter mixture into the dry ingredients until combined. Add the eggs and mix well until smooth. Pour the mixture into the prepared tin and smooth out the surface.

Bake for 1–1 hour 15 minutes, or until a skewer comes out clean when inserted into the centre of the cake. Let the cake cool in the tin for 1 hour before turning out onto a wire rack. Dust the cake with cocoa powder and icing sugar and serve warm with whipped cream.

pies, tarts and pastries

Tarte au Citron

✦ SERVES 6–8
✦ PREPARATION TIME: 1 HOUR +
✦ COOKING TIME: 1 HOUR 40 MINUTES

PASTRY
125 g (4½ oz/1 cup) plain (all-purpose)
    flour
80 g (2¾ oz) unsalted butter, softened
1 egg yolk
2 tablespoons icing (confectioners')
    sugar, sifted

3 eggs
2 egg yolks
175 g (6 oz/¾ cup) caster (superfine)
    sugar
125 ml (4 fl oz/½ cup) cream
185 ml (6 fl oz/¾ cup) lemon juice
1½ tablespoons finely grated lemon zest
2 small lemons
140 g (5 oz/⅔ cup) sugar

To make the pastry, sift the flour and a pinch of salt into a large bowl. Make a well in the centre and add the butter, egg yolk and icing sugar. Work together the butter, yolk and sugar with your fingertips, then slowly incorporate the flour. Bring together into a ball — you may need to add a few drops of cold water. Flatten the ball slightly, cover with plastic wrap and refrigerate for 20 minutes.

Preheat the oven to 200°C (400°F/Gas 6). Grease a shallow loose-based flan (tart) tin, 2 cm (¾ inch) deep and 21 cm (8¼ inch) across the base.

Roll out the pastry between two sheets of baking paper until it is 3 mm (⅛ inch) thick, to fit the base and side of the tin. Trim the edge. Refrigerate for 10 minutes. Line the pastry with baking paper and spread baking beads or uncooked rice over. Bake for 10 minutes. Remove the paper and beads and bake for another 6–8 minutes, or until the pastry looks dry all over. Cool the pastry and reduce the oven to 150°C (300°F/Gas 2).

Whisk the eggs, egg yolks and sugar together, add the cream and lemon juice and mix well. Strain and then add the lemon zest. Place the flan tin on a baking sheet on the middle shelf of the oven and carefully pour in the filling right up to the top. Bake for 40 minutes, or until it is just set — it should wobble in the middle when the tin is firmly tapped. Cool the tart before removing from its tin.

Meanwhile, wash and scrub the lemons well. Slice very thinly (2 mm/1/16 inch thick). Combine the sugar and 200 ml (7 fl oz) water in a small frying pan and stir over low heat until the sugar has dissolved. Add the lemon slices and simmer over low heat for 40 minutes, or until the peel is very tender and the pith looks transparent. Lift out of the syrup and drain on baking paper. If serving the tart immediately, cover the surface with the lemon slices. If not, keep the slices covered and decorate the tart when ready to serve. Serve warm or chilled, with a little cream.

Butterscotch Tart

🌲 SERVES 6–8

🌲 PREPARATION TIME: 30 MINUTES +

🌲 COOKING TIME: 1 HOUR

SHORTCRUST PASTRY

250 g (9 oz/2 cups) plain (all-purpose)
    flour
125 g (4½ oz) unsalted butter, chilled and
    chopped
2 tablespoons caster (superfine) sugar
1 egg yolk
1 tablespoon iced water

BUTTERSCOTCH FILLING

185 g (6½ oz/1 cup) soft brown sugar
40 g (1½ oz/⅓ cup) plain (all-purpose)
    flour
250 ml (9 fl oz/1 cup) milk
50 g (1¾ oz) unsalted butter
1 teaspoon natural vanilla extract
1 egg yolk

MERINGUE

2 egg whites
2 tablespoons caster (superfine) sugar

Preheat the oven to 180°C (350°F/Gas 4). Grease a
deep 22 cm (8½ inch) flan (tart) tin. Sift the flour into
a large bowl. Using your fingertips, rub in the butter
until the mixture resembles fine breadcrumbs. Stir in
the sugar, egg yolk and iced water. Mix to a soft dough
with a flat-bladed knife, using a cutting action, then
gather into a ball. Wrap and refrigerate for 20 minutes.

Roll the pastry between two sheets of baking paper,
large enough to cover the base and side of the tin.
Trim the edge and prick the pastry evenly with a fork.
Refrigerate for 20 minutes. Line the pastry with baking
paper and spread baking beads or uncooked rice over
the paper. Bake for 35 minutes, then remove the paper
and beads.

To make the filling, place the sugar and flour in a
small saucepan. Make a well in the centre and
gradually whisk in the milk to form a smooth paste.
Add the butter and stir with a whisk over low heat for
8 minutes, or until the mixture boils and thickens.
Remove from the heat, add the vanilla extract and
egg yolk and whisk until smooth. Spread into the
pastry case and smooth the surface.

To make the meringue, beat the egg whites until firm
peaks form. Add the sugar gradually, beating until
thick and glossy and all the sugar has dissolved.
Spoon over the filling and swirl into peaks with a
fork or flat-bladed knife. Bake for 5–10 minutes,
or until the meringue is golden. Serve warm or cold.

Millefeuille with Passionfruit Curd

🌿 SERVES 4
🌿 PREPARATION TIME: 30 MINUTES +
🌿 COOKING TIME: 45 MINUTES

PASSIONFRUIT CURD

3 eggs
60 g (2¼ oz) unsalted butter
125 g (4½ oz/½ cup) passionfruit pulp
110 g (3¾ oz/½ cup) sugar

500 g (1 lb 2 oz) block ready-made puff
    pastry, thawed
300 ml (10½ fl oz) whipped cream
2 tablespoons icing (confectioners') sugar
1 teaspoon natural vanilla extract
1 large mango, thinly sliced
sifted icing (confectioners') sugar, plus
    extra, to sprinkle

To make the passionfruit curd, beat the eggs well, then strain into a heatproof bowl and add the remaining ingredients. Place the bowl over a saucepan of simmering water and stir with a wooden spoon for 15–20 minutes, or until the butter has melted and the mixture has thickened slightly and coats the back of the wooden spoon. Cool, then transfer to a bowl, cover with plastic wrap and chill until required.

To make the millefeuille, preheat the oven to 200°C (400°F/Gas 6). Line a large baking tray with baking paper. Roll the pastry to a 30 x 35 cm (12 x 14 inch) rectangle and transfer to the tray. Cover and refrigerate for 20 minutes. Sprinkle lightly with water and prick all over with a fork. Cook for 25 minutes, or until puffed and golden. Allow to cool completely on a wire rack.

Whisk the cream with the icing sugar and vanilla extract until firm peaks form. Carefully trim the pastry sheet and cut lengthways into three even-sized strips. Spread one layer of pastry with half the passionfruit curd, spreading evenly to the edges. Top this with half of the whipped cream and then top with half of the mango flesh. Place a second sheet of pastry on top and repeat the process. Top with the remaining pastry sheet and sprinkle liberally with icing sugar. Carefully transfer to a serving plate. Use a serrated knife to cut into slices.

NOTE: Instead of making one long millefeuille, you might prefer to make four individual ones.

Lemon Meringue Pie

185 g (6½ oz/1½ cups) plain
   (all-purpose) flour
2 tablespoons icing (confectioners') sugar
125 g (4½ oz) chilled unsalted butter,
   chopped
60 ml (2 fl oz/¼ cup) iced water

FILLING AND TOPPING
30 g (1 oz/¼ cup) cornflour (cornstarch)
30 g (1 oz/¼ cup) plain (all-purpose)
   flour
230 g (8½ oz/1 cup) caster (superfine)
   sugar
185 ml (6 fl oz/¾ cup) lemon juice
3 teaspoons grated lemon zest
40 g (1½ oz) unsalted butter, chopped
6 eggs, separated
350 g (12 oz/1½ cups) caster (superfine)
   sugar, extra
½ teaspoon cornflour (cornstarch), extra

Sift the flour and icing sugar into a large bowl. Using your fingertips, rub in the butter until the mixture resembles fine breadcrumbs. Add almost all the water and mix with a flat-bladed knife, using a cutting action, until the mixture forms a firm dough. Add more liquid if the dough is too dry. Turn onto a lightly floured surface and gather together into a ball. Roll between two sheets of baking paper until large enough to fit a 23 cm (9 inch) pie dish. Line the pie dish with the pastry, trim the edge and refrigerate for 20 minutes. Preheat the oven to 180°C (350°F/Gas 4).

Line the pastry with a sheet of baking paper and spread a layer of baking beads or uncooked rice evenly over the paper. Bake for 10 minutes, then remove the paper and beads. Bake for a further 10 minutes, or until the pastry is lightly golden. Leave to cool.

To make the filling, put the flours and sugar in a saucepan. Whisk in the lemon juice, zest and 375 ml (13 oz/1½ cups) water. Whisk continually over medium heat until the mixture boils and thickens. Reduce the heat and cook for 1 minute, then whisk in the butter and egg yolks, one yolk at a time. Transfer to a bowl, cover the surface with plastic wrap and allow to cool completely.

To make the topping, preheat the oven to 220°C (425°F/Gas 7). Beat the egg whites in a clean, dry bowl using electric beaters, until soft peaks form. Add the extra sugar gradually, beating constantly until the meringue is thick and glossy. Beat in the extra cornflour. Pour the cold filling into the cold pastry shell. Spread with meringue to cover, forming peaks. Bake for 5–10 minutes, or until lightly browned. Serve hot or cold.

Chocolate Collar Cheesecake

🔺 SERVES 8–10

🔺 PREPARATION TIME: 1 HOUR 30 MINUTES +

🔺 COOKING TIME: 50 MINUTES

200 g (7 oz) plain chocolate biscuits
   (cookies), crushed
70 g (2½ oz) unsalted butter, melted
500 g (1 lb 2 oz/2 cups) cream cheese,
   softened
75 g (2¾ oz/⅓ cup) sugar
2 eggs
1 tablespoon unsweetened cocoa powder
300 g (10½ oz) sour cream
250 g (9 oz) dark chocolate, melted and
   cooked
80 ml (2½ fl oz/⅓ cup) Bailey's Irish
   Cream
50 g (1¾ oz) white chocolate, melted
150 g (5½ oz) dark chocolate, melted
310 ml (10¾ fl oz/1¼ cups) whipped
   cream
unsweetened cocoa powder and icing
   (confectioners') sugar, to dust

Brush a 23 cm (9 inch) round spring-form cake tin with melted butter and line the base and side with baking paper. Mix together the biscuit crumbs and butter, press firmly into the base of the tin and refrigerate for 10 minutes. Preheat the oven to 180°C (350°F/Gas 4).

Beat the cream cheese and sugar using electric beaters until smooth and creamy. Add the eggs, one at a time, beating thoroughly after each addition. Beat in the cocoa and sour cream until smooth. Beat in the cooled melted dark chocolate. Beat in the liqueur and pour over the base. Smooth the surface and bake for about 45 minutes. The cheesecake may not be fully set, but will firm up. Refrigerate until cold.

Remove the cheesecake from the tin and put it on a board. Measure the height and add 5 mm (¼ inch). Cut a strip of baking paper this wide and 75 cm (29½ inches) long.

Pipe or drizzle the melted white chocolate in a figure eight pattern along the paper. When just set, spread the dark chocolate over the entire strip of paper. Allow the chocolate to set a little, but you need to be able to bend the paper without it cracking. Wrap the paper around the cheesecake with the chocolate inside. Seal the ends and hold the paper in place until the chocolate is completely set. Peel away the paper. Spread the top with cream, then dust with cocoa and icing sugar.

Galette des Rois

⚶ MAKES 1

⚶ PREPARATION TIME: 25 MINUTES +

⚶ COOKING TIME: 35 MINUTES

2 x 375 g (12 oz) blocks ready-made puff
    pastry, thawed
75 g (2$\frac{1}{2}$ oz/$\frac{3}{4}$ cup) ground almonds
90 g (3$\frac{1}{4}$ oz/$\frac{1}{3}$ cup) caster (superfine)
    sugar or vanilla sugar
1 tablespoon cornflour (cornstarch)
1 teaspoon finely grated orange zest
100 g (3$\frac{1}{2}$ oz) unsalted butter, softened
3 egg yolks
$\frac{1}{2}$ teaspoon natural almond extract
1 tablespoon rum or Kirsch
1 dried haricot bean or ceramic token
1 egg, lightly beaten, for glazing

Roll out one block of pastry on a lightly floured surface to 5 mm ($\frac{1}{4}$ inch) thick and cut into a 22 cm (9 inch) circle. Repeat with the other block of pastry. Line a baking tray with baking paper and top with one of the circles.

In a bowl, combine the almonds, sugar, cornflour and zest. Add the butter, egg yolks, almond and rum or Kirsch and mix well. Spread over the pastry on the tray, poking in the bean or token in the centre and leaving a 2 cm ($\frac{3}{4}$ inch) rim. Brush the rim with some beaten egg, taking care not to brush the cut edges as this will prevent the pastry from puffing.

Place the second circle of puff pastry over the first, pressing gently around the edge to seal. Using a sharp knife, make swirling patterns from the centre, fanning outwards in the pastry, taking care not to cut all the way through. Brush the top with beaten egg and refrigerate for 30 minutes. Preheat the oven to 200°C (400°F/Gas 6). Bake for 30–35 minutes, or until well puffed and golden. Serve warm or cold.

Sables with Berries and Cream

⚜ SERVES 6

⚜ PREPARATION TIME: 50 MINUTES

⚜ COOKING TIME: 50 MINUTES

185 g (6½ oz/1½ cups) plain
    (all-purpose) flour
40 g (1½ oz/⅓ cup) icing
    (confectioners') sugar
125 g (4½ oz) unsalted butter, chilled
    and chopped
1 egg yolk
1 tablespoon lemon juice
375 ml (13 fl oz/1½ cups) whipping
    cream
1 teaspoon natural vanilla extract
1 tablespoon icing (confectioners')
    sugar, extra
400 g (14 oz) mixed berries
icing (confectioners') sugar, to dust

Preheat the oven to 160°C (315°F/Gas 2–3). Grease two baking trays and line with baking paper. Sift the flour and icing sugar into a bowl. With your fingertips, rub the butter into the flour until fine and crumbly. Make a well in the centre, add the egg yolk and lemon juice and mix to a dough with a knife. Gather into a ball, cover and refrigerate for 15 minutes.

Divide the dough in half. Roll out one half between well-floured sheets of baking paper to 3 mm (⅛ inch) thick. Slide the pastry onto a tray and refrigerate for 5–10 minutes. Using a 7.5 cm (3 inch) round or heart-shaped biscuit (cookie) cutter dipped in flour, cut out nine shapes. Carefully place on the prepared trays, prick with a fork and refrigerate for 10 minutes. Bake for 20–25 minutes, or until the biscuits are firm but not coloured. Allow to cool slightly on the tray before transferring to a wire rack to cool completely. Repeat with the remaining dough.

Whisk the cream, vanilla extract and extra icing sugar together until firm. Spoon or pipe the cream mixture on top of six of the biscuits. Top with some berries. Add a second biscuit and repeat with the cream and berries. Finish by adding a third biscuit to the top. Lightly dust with icing sugar.

Sicilian Cannoli

🔸 MAKES 12
🔸 PREPARATION TIME: 30 MINUTES +
🔸 COOKING TIME: 5 MINUTES

FILLING
500 g (1 lb 2 oz) ricotta cheese
1 teaspoon orange flower water
100 g (3½ oz/½ cup) cedro, diced
    (see Notes)
60 g (2¼ oz) bittersweet chocolate,
    coarsely grated or chopped
1 tablespoon grated orange zest
60 g (2¼ oz/½ cup) icing
    (confectioners') sugar

300 g (10½ oz) plain (all-purpose) flour
1 tablespoon caster (superfine) sugar
1 teaspoon ground cinnamon
40 g (1½ oz) unsalted butter
60 ml (2 fl oz/¼ cup) Marsala
vegetable oil, for deep-frying
icing (confectioners') sugar, to dust

To make the filling, combine all the ingredients in a bowl and mix. Set aside.

Combine the flour, sugar and cinnamon in a bowl, rub in the butter and add the Marsala. Mix until the dough comes together in a loose clump, then knead on a lightly floured surface for 4–5 minutes, or until smooth. Wrap in plastic wrap and refrigerate for at least 30 minutes.

Cut the dough in half and roll each portion on a lightly floured surface into a thin sheet about 5 mm (¼ inch) thick. Cut each dough half into six 9 cm (3½ inch) squares. Place a metal tube (see Note) diagonally across the middle of each square. Fold the sides over the tube, moistening the overlap with water, then press together.

Heat the oil in a large deep frying pan to 180°C (350°F), or until a cube of bread dropped into the oil browns in 15 seconds. Drop one or two tubes at a time into the hot oil. Fry gently until golden brown and crisp. Remove from the oil, gently remove the moulds and drain on crumpled paper towels. When they are cool, fill a piping (icing) bag with the ricotta mixture and fill the shells. Dust with icing sugar and serve.

NOTES: Cedro, also known as citron, is a citrus fruit with a very thick, knobbly skin. The skin is used to make candied peel.
    Cannoli tubes are available at kitchenware shops. You can also use 2 cm (¾ inch) diameter wooden dowels cut into 12 cm (4½ inch) lengths.

Pumpkin Pie

🔺 SERVES 8

🔺 PREPARATION TIME: 20 MINUTES +

🔺 COOKING TIME: 1 HOUR 10 MINUTES

FILLING

500 g (1 lb 2 oz) pumpkin (winter
　squash), chopped into small chunks
2 eggs, lightly beaten
140 g (5 oz/3/4 cup) soft brown sugar
80 ml (2 1/2 fl oz/1/3 cup) cream
1 tablespoon sweet sherry
1 teaspoon ground cinnamon
1/2 teaspoon freshly grated nutmeg
1/2 teaspoon ground ginger

PASTRY

150 g (5 1/2 oz/1 1/4 cups) plain
　(all-purpose) flour
100 g (3 1/2 oz) unsalted butter, cubed
2 teaspoons caster (superfine) sugar
80 ml (2 1/2 fl oz/1/3 cup) iced water
1 egg yolk, lightly beaten, to glaze
1 tablespoon milk, to glaze

Lightly grease a 23 cm (9 inch) round pie dish. Steam or boil the pumpkin for 10 minutes, or until just tender. Drain the pumpkin thoroughly, then mash and set aside to cool.

To make the pastry, sift the flour into a large bowl. Using your fingertips, rub in the butter until the mixture resembles fine breadcrumbs. Stir in the caster sugar. Make a well in the centre, add almost all the water and mix with a flat-bladed knife, using a cutting action, until the mixture comes together in beads. Add the remaining water if the dough is too dry.

Gather the dough together and roll out between two sheets of baking paper until large enough to cover the base and side of the pie dish. Line the dish with pastry, trim away the excess pastry and crimp the edges. Roll out the pastry trimmings to 2 mm (1/16 inch) thick. Using a sharp knife, cut out leaf shapes of different sizes and score vein markings onto the leaves. Refrigerate the pastry-lined dish and the leaf shapes for about 20 minutes.

Preheat the oven to 180°C (350°F/Gas 4). Cut baking paper to cover the pastry-lined dish. Spread baking beads or uncooked rice over the paper. Bake for 10 minutes, remove the paper and beads and bake for another 10 minutes, or until lightly golden. Meanwhile, place the leaves on a baking tray lined with baking paper, brush with the combined egg yolk and milk and bake for 10–15 minutes, or until lightly golden. Set aside to cool.

To make the filling, whisk the eggs and brown sugar in a large bowl. Add the cooled mashed pumpkin, cream, sherry, cinnamon, nutmeg and ginger and stir to combine thoroughly. Pour the filling into the pastry shell, smooth the surface with the back of a spoon, then bake for 40 minutes, or until set. If the pastry edges begin to brown too much during cooking, cover the edges with foil. Allow the pie to cool to room temperature and then decorate the top with the leaves. Pumpkin pie can be served with ice cream or whipped cream.

Paris Brest

🌾 SERVES 6–8

🌾 PREPARATION TIME: 50 MINUTES

🌾 COOKING TIME: 1 HOUR 15 MINUTES

CHOUX PASTRY

50 g (1¾ oz) unsalted butter

90 g (3¼ oz/¾ cup) plain (all-purpose) flour, sifted

3 eggs, lightly beaten

FILLING

3 egg yolks

55 g (2 oz/¼ cup) caster (superfine) sugar

2 tablespoons plain (all-purpose) flour

250 ml (9 fl oz/1 cup) milk

1 teaspoon natural vanilla extract

250 ml (9 fl oz/1 cup) whipping cream, whipped

200 g (7 oz) raspberries or 250 g (9 oz) strawberries, halved, or a mixture of both

TOPPING

125 g (4½ oz) dark chocolate, chopped

30 g (1 oz) unsalted butter

1 tablespoon whipped cream

Preheat the oven to 210°C (415°F/Gas 6–7). Brush a large tray with melted butter or oil and line the tray with baking paper. Mark a 23 cm (9 inch) circle on the paper.

To make the pastry, stir the butter with 185 ml (6 fl oz/¾ cup) water in a saucepan over low heat until the butter has melted and the mixture boils. Remove from the heat, add the flour all at once and, using a wooden spoon, beat until smooth. Return to the heat and beat until the mixture thickens and comes away from the side of the pan. Remove from the heat and cool slightly. Transfer to a large bowl. Using electric beaters, add the eggs gradually, beating until stiff and glossy. Place heaped tablespoons of mixture touching each other, using the marked circle as a guide. Bake for 25–30 minutes, or until browned and hollow sounding when the base is tapped. Turn off the oven and leave the pastry to dry in the oven.

To make the filling, whisk the egg yolks, sugar and flour in a bowl until pale. Heat the milk in a saucepan until almost boiling. Gradually add to the egg mixture, stirring constantly. Return to the pan and stir constantly over medium heat until the mixture boils and thickens. Cook for another 2 minutes, stirring constantly. Remove from the heat and stir in the vanilla extract. Transfer to a bowl, cover the surface with plastic wrap to prevent a skin forming and set aside to cool.

To make the topping, combine all the ingredients in a heatproof bowl. Stand the bowl over a saucepan of simmering water, making sure the base doesn't tough the water, and stir until the chocolate has melted and the mixture is smooth. Cool slightly.

To assemble, cut the pastry ring in half horizontally using a serrated knife. Remove any excess dough that remains in the centre. Fold the whipped cream through the custard and spoon into the base of the pastry. Top with the fruit. Replace the remaining pastry half on top. Spread the chocolate mixture over the top. Leave to set.

Raspberry Shortcake

⚜ SERVES 6–8

⚜ PREPARATION TIME: 30 MINUTES +

⚜ COOKING TIME: 35 MINUTES

PASTRY

125 g (4 1/2 oz/1 cup) plain (all-purpose)
    flour
40 g (1 1/2 oz/1/3 cup) icing
    (confectioners') sugar
90 g (3 1/4 oz) chilled unsalted
    butter, chopped
1 egg yolk
1/2 teaspoon natural vanilla extract
1/2–1 tablespoon iced water

TOPPING

750 g (1 lb 10 oz/6 cups) fresh
    raspberries
30 g (1 oz/1/4 cup) icing
    (confectioners') sugar
110 g (3 3/4 oz/1/3 cup) redcurrant jelly
cream, to serve

To make the pastry, sift the flour and icing sugar into a large bowl. Using your fingertips, rub in the butter until the mixture resembles fine breadcrumbs. Add the egg yolk, vanilla extract and enough of the iced water to make the ingredients come together, then mix to a dough with a flat-bladed knife, using a cutting action. Turn out onto a lightly floured work surface and gather together into a ball. Flatten slightly, wrap in plastic wrap and refrigerate for 30 minutes.

Preheat the oven to 180°C (350°F/Gas 4). Roll out the pastry to fit a fluted 10 x 34 cm (4 x 13 1/2 inch) loose-based flan (tart) tin and trim the edge. Prick all over with a fork and refrigerate for 20 minutes. Line the pastry with baking paper and spread a layer of baking beads or uncooked rice evenly over the paper. Bake for 15–20 minutes, or until golden. Remove the paper and beads and bake for another 15 minutes. Cool on a wire rack.

To make the topping, set aside 500 g (1 lb 2 oz/4 cups) of the best raspberries and mash the rest with the icing sugar. Evenly spread the mashed raspberries over the shortcake just before serving.

Cover with the whole raspberries. Heat the redcurrant jelly in a small saucepan until melted and smooth. Use a soft pastry brush to coat the raspberries heavily with warm glaze. Cut into slices and serve with cream.

NOTE: Strawberry shortcake is a classic American dish. It is usually made as a round of shortcake which is split, then filled or topped with fresh strawberries.

Apple Tarte Tatin

SERVES 6

PREPARATION TIME: 30 MINUTES +

COOKING TIME: 55 MINUTES

210 g (7 1/2 oz/1 2/3 cups) plain
    (all-purpose) flour
125 g (4 1/2 oz) unsalted butter, chilled and
    cubed
2 tablespoons caster (superfine) sugar
1 egg, lightly beaten
2 drops natural vanilla extract
8 granny smith apples
110 g (3 3/4 oz/1/2 cup) sugar
40 g (1 1/2 oz) unsalted butter, extra,
    chopped
cream or ice cream, to serve

Sift the flour into a bowl. Using your fingertips, rub in the butter until the mixture resembles fine breadcrumbs. Stir in the caster sugar, then make a well in the centre. Add the egg and vanilla extract and mix with a flat-bladed knife, using a cutting action, until the mixture comes together in beads. Gather the dough together, then turn out onto a lightly floured work surface and shape into a round. Wrap in plastic wrap and refrigerate for at least 30 minutes, to firm.

Peel and core the apples and cut each into eight slices. Put the sugar and 1 tablespoon water in a heavy-based 25 cm (10 inch) frying pan that has a metal or removable handle, so that it can safely be placed in the oven. Stir over low heat for 1 minute, or until the sugar has dissolved. Increase the heat to medium and cook for 4–5 minutes, or until the caramel turns golden. Add the extra butter and stir to incorporate. Remove from the heat.

Place the apple slices in neat circles to cover the base of the frying pan. Return the pan to low heat and cook for 10–12 minutes, or until the apples are tender and caramelized. Remove the pan from the heat and leave to cool for 10 minutes.

Preheat the oven to 220°C (425°F/Gas 7). Roll the pastry out on a lightly floured surface to a circle 1 cm (1/2 in) larger than the frying pan. Place the pastry over the apples to cover them completely, tucking it down firmly at the edges. Bake for 30–35 minutes, or until the pastry is cooked. Leave for 15 minutes before turning out onto a plate. Serve warm or cold with cream or ice cream.

NOTE: Special high-sided tatin tins are available from speciality kitchenware shops.

Pecan Pie

⋏ SERVES 6
⋏ PREPARATION TIME: 30 MINUTES +
⋏ COOKING TIME: 1 HOUR 15 MINUTES

SHORTCRUST PASTRY

185 g (6½ oz/1½ cups) plain
  (all-purpose) flour
125 g (4½ oz) chilled unsalted butter,
  chopped
2–3 tablespoons chilled water

FILLING

200 g (7 oz/2 cups) pecans
3 eggs, lightly beaten
50 g (1¾ oz) unsalted butter, melted
  and cooled
140 g (5 oz/¾ cup) soft brown sugar
170 ml (5½ fl oz/⅔ cup) light corn syrup
1 teaspoon natural vanilla extract

Preheat the oven to 180°C (350°F/Gas 4). Sift the flour into a large bowl. Using your fingertips, rub in the butter until the mixture resembles fine breadcrumbs. Add almost all the water and mix with a flat-bladed knife, using a cutting action, until the mixture comes together in beads. Add more water if the dough is too dry. Turn out onto a lightly floured work surface and gather together into a ball.

Roll out the pastry to a 35 cm (14 in) round. Line a 23 cm (9 in) flan (tart) tin with pastry, trim the edges and refrigerate for 20 minutes. Gather the pastry trimmings together, roll out on baking paper to a rectangle about 2 mm (¹⁄₁₆ in) thick, then refrigerate.

Line the pastry-lined tin with a sheet of baking paper and spread a layer of baking beads or uncooked rice evenly over the paper. Bake for 15 minutes, remove the paper and beads and bake for another 15 minutes, or until lightly golden. Cool completely.

Spread the pecans over the pastry base. Whisk together the eggs, butter, sugar, corn syrup, vanilla extract and a pinch of salt until well combined, then pour over the nuts.

Using a fluted pastry wheel or small sharp knife, cut narrow strips from half of the pastry trimmings. Cut out small leaves and stars with biscuit (cookie) cutters from the remaining trimmings. Arrange over the filling. Bake the pie for 45 minutes, or until firm. Allow to cool completely and serve at room temperature.

Fruit Tart

🔺 SERVES 6
🔺 PREPARATION TIME: 40 MINUTES +
🔺 COOKING TIME: 40 MINUTES

SHORTCRUST PASTRY

150 g (5½ oz/1¼ cups) plain
    (all-purpose) flour
2 tablespoons caster (superfine) sugar
90 g (3¼ oz) chilled unsalted butter,
    chopped
1 egg yolk
1 tablespoon iced water

FILLING

250 ml (9 fl oz/1 cup) milk
3 egg yolks
55 g (2 oz/¼ cup) caster (superfine)
    sugar
2 tablespoons plain (all-purpose) flour
1 teaspoon natural vanilla extract
strawberries, kiwi fruit and blueberries,
    to decorate
apricot jam, to glaze

Sift the flour into a bowl and stir in the sugar. Using your fingertips, rub in the butter until the mixture resembles fine breadcrumbs. Make a well in the centre and add the egg yolk and iced water. Mix to a dough with a flat-bladed knife, using a cutting action. Turn out onto a lightly floured work surface and gather together into a ball. Press together gently until smooth, and then roll out to fit a 10 x 34 cm (4 x 13½ inch) loose-based fluted flan (tart) tin. Line the tin with pastry and trim away any excess. Wrap in plastic wrap and refrigerate for 20 minutes. Preheat the oven to 190°C (375°F/Gas 5).

Line the pastry-lined tin with baking paper and spread a layer of baking beads or uncooked rice evenly over the paper. Bake for 15 minutes, remove the paper and beads and bake for another 20 minutes, or until cooked on the base and golden brown around the edge. Set aside to cool completely.

To make the filling, put the milk into a small saucepan and bring to the boil. Set aside while quickly whisking the egg yolks and sugar together in a bowl, until light and creamy. Whisk in the flour. Pour the hot milk slowly onto the egg mixture, whisking constantly. Wash out the pan, return the milk mixture to the pan and bring to the boil over medium heat, stirring with a wire whisk. Boil for 2 minutes, stirring occasionally. Transfer to a bowl, stir in the vanilla extract, and leave to cool, stirring frequently to avoid a skin forming. When cooled to room temperature, cover the surface with plastic wrap and refrigerate until cold.

Cut the strawberries in half and peel and slice the kiwi fruit. Spoon the cold custard into the cold pastry shell, then arrange all the fruit over the custard, pressing in slightly. Heat the jam in the microwave or in a small saucepan until liquid, sieve to remove any lumps, then, using a pastry brush, glaze the fruit with the jam. Serve the tart on the same day, at room temperature. If it is to be left for a while on a hot day, refrigerate it.

New York Cheesecake

🌲 SERVES 10–12

🌲 PREPARATION TIME: 1 HOUR +

🌲 COOKING TIME: 1 HOUR 50 MINUTES

60 g (2¼ oz/½ cup) self-raising flour
125 g (4½ oz/1 cup) plain
   (all-purpose) flour
55 g (2 oz/¼ cup) caster (superfine)
   sugar
1 teaspoon grated lemon zest
80 g (2¾ oz) unsalted butter, chopped
1 egg
375 ml (13 fl oz/1½ cups) cream,
   to serve

FILLING
750 g (1 lb 10 oz/3 cups) cream cheese,
   softened
230 g (8½ oz/1 cup) caster (superfine)
   sugar
30 g (1 oz/¼ cup) plain (all-purpose)
   flour
2 teaspoons grated orange zest
2 teaspoons grated lemon zest
4 eggs
170 ml (5½ fl oz/⅔ cup) whipping cream

CANDIED ZEST
finely shredded zest of 3 limes, 3 lemons
   and 3 oranges
230 g (8½ oz/1 cup) caster (superfine)
   sugar

Preheat the oven to 210°C (415°F/Gas 6–7). Lightly grease a 23 cm (9 in) spring-form cake tin.

To make the pastry, combine the flours, sugar, lemon zest and butter for about 30 seconds in a food processor, until crumbly. Add the egg and process briefly until the mixture just comes together. Turn out onto a lightly floured surface and gather together into a ball. Refrigerate in plastic wrap for about 20 minutes, or until the mixture is firm.

Roll the dough between two sheets of baking paper until large enough to fit the base and side of the tin. Ease into the tin and trim the edges. Cover the pastry with baking paper, then baking beads or uncooked rice. Bake for 10 minutes, then remove the baking paper and beads. Flatten the pastry lightly with the back of a spoon and bake for another 5 minutes. Set aside to cool.

To make the filling, reduce the oven to 150°C (300°F/Gas 2). Beat the cream cheese, sugar, flour and orange and lemon zest until smooth. Add the eggs, one at a time, beating after each addition. Beat in the cream, pour over the pastry and bake for 1½ hours, or until almost set. Leave to cool, then refrigerate.

To make the candied zest, place a little water in a saucepan with the lime, lemon and orange zest, bring to the boil and simmer for 1 minute. Drain the zest and repeat with fresh water. This will get rid of any bitterness in the zest and syrup. Put the sugar in a saucepan with 60 ml (2 fl oz/¼ cup) water and stir over low heat until dissolved. Add the zest, bring to the boil, reduce the heat and simmer for 5–6 minutes, or until the zest looks translucent. Allow to cool, drain the zest and place on baking paper to dry (you can save the syrup to serve with the cheesecake). Whip the cream, spoon over the cold cheesecake and top with candied zest.

NOTE: To make the cheesecake easier to cut, heap the zest in mounds, then cut between the mounds of zest.

Cherry Pie

🔺 SERVES 6–8

🔺 PREPARATION TIME: 25 MINUTES +

🔺 COOKING TIME: 40 MINUTES

150 g (5½ oz/1¼ cups) plain
(all-purpose) flour
30 g (1 oz/¼ cup) icing (confectioners')
sugar
100 g (3½ oz) chilled unsalted butter,
chopped
60 g (2¼ oz) ground almonds
60 ml (2 fl oz/¼ cup) iced water
2 x 700 g (1 lb 9 oz) tinned pitted morello
cherries, drained
1 egg, lightly beaten, to glaze
caster (superfine) sugar, to sprinkle
ice cream or cream (optional), to serve

To make the pastry, sift the flour and icing sugar into a bowl. Using your fingertips, rub in the butter until the mixture resembles fine breadcrumbs. Stir in the ground almonds, then add almost all the water. Mix with a flat-bladed knife, using a cutting action, until the mixture forms a dough. Add the remaining water if the dough is too dry.

Turn the dough onto a lightly floured work surface and gather together into a ball. Roll out on a sheet of baking paper into a circle about 26 cm (10½ inches) in diameter. Flatten slightly, cover with plastic wrap and refrigerate for 20 minutes. Spread the cherries into a 23 cm (9 inch) round pie dish.

Preheat the oven to 200°C (400°F/Gas 6). Cover the pie dish with the pastry and trim the overhanging edge. Roll out the remaining scraps of pastry and use a small sharp knife to cut out decorations. Brush the pastry top all over with beaten egg and arrange the decorations on top. Brush these with beaten egg as well, and then sprinkle lightly with caster sugar. Place the pie dish on a baking tray (the cherry juice may overflow a little) and cook for 35–40 minutes, or until golden brown. Serve with ice cream or cream.

Pear and Almond Flan

🔺 SERVES 8

🔺 PREPARATION TIME: 15 MINUTES +

🔺 COOKING TIME: 1 HOUR 10 MINUTES

PASTRY

150 g (5$\frac{1}{2}$ oz/1$\frac{1}{4}$ cups) plain
   (all-purpose) flour
90 g (3$\frac{1}{4}$ oz) unsalted butter, chilled and
   cubed
55 g (2 oz/$\frac{1}{4}$ cup) caster (superfine)
   sugar
2 egg yolks, lightly beaten

FILLING

165 g (5$\frac{3}{4}$ oz) unsalted butter, softened
150 g (5$\frac{1}{2}$ oz/$\frac{2}{3}$ cup) caster (superfine)
   sugar
3 eggs
125 g (4$\frac{1}{2}$ oz/1$\frac{1}{4}$ cups) ground almonds
1$\frac{1}{2}$ tablespoons plain (all-purpose) flour
2 very ripe pears

Lightly grease a shallow 24 cm (9$\frac{1}{2}$ inch) round, loose-based, fluted flan (tart) tin.

To make the pastry, sift the flour into a bowl. Using your fingertips, rub in the butter until the mixture resembles fine breadcrumbs. Stir in the caster sugar and mix together. Make a well in the centre, add the egg yolks and mix with a flat-bladed knife, using a cutting action, until the mixture comes together in beads. Turn out onto a lightly floured work surface and gather into a ball. Wrap in plastic wrap and refrigerate for 30 minutes.

Preheat the oven to 180°C (350°F/Gas 4). Roll out the pastry between two sheets of baking paper until large enough to line the base and side of the tin. Line the tin with the pastry and trim the edge. Sparsely prick the base with a fork. Line the base with baking paper and spread some baking beads or uncooked rice evenly over the pastry. Bake for 10 minutes. Remove the paper and beads and bake for another 10 minutes. Cool.

To make the filling, beat the butter and sugar in a bowl using electric beaters for 30 seconds (don't cream the mixture). Add the eggs one at a time, beating after each addition. Fold in the ground almonds and flour and spread the filling smoothly over the cooled pastry base.

Peel the pears, halve lengthways and remove the cores. Cut crossways into 3 mm ($\frac{1}{8}$ inch) slices. Separate the slices slightly, then place the slices on top of the tart to form a cross. Bake for about 50 minutes, or until the filling has set (the middle may still be a little soft). Cool in the tin, then refrigerate for at least 2 hours before serving. Dust with icing sugar before serving.

Summer Berry Tart

🌲 SERVES 4–6
🌲 PREPARATION TIME: 35 MINUTES +
🌲 COOKING TIME: 35 MINUTES

PASTRY
125 g (4½ oz/1 cup) plain
   (all-purpose) flour
90 g (3¼ oz) chilled unsalted butter,
   cubed
2 tablespoons icing (confectioners') sugar
1–2 tablespoons iced water

FILLING
3 egg yolks
2 tablespoons caster (superfine) sugar
2 tablespoons cornflour (cornstarch)
250 ml (9 fl oz/1 cup) milk
1 teaspoon natural vanilla extract
250 g (9 oz/1⅔ cups) strawberries, hulled
   and halved
125 g (4½ oz/1 cup) blueberries
125 g (4½ oz/1 cup) raspberries
2 tablespoons apricot jam (see Note)

Preheat the oven to 180°C (350°F/Gas 4). Lightly grease a 20 cm (8 inch) round, loose-based, fluted flan (tart) tin.

To make the pastry, sift the flour into a bowl. Using your fingertips, rub in the butter until the mixture resembles fine breadcrumbs. Mix in the icing sugar. Make a well in the centre and add almost all the water. Mix with a flat-bladed knife, using a cutting action, until the mixture comes together in beads. Add more water if the dough is too dry.

Roll out the pastry between two sheets of baking paper to fit the base and side of the tin. Line the tin with the pastry and trim away any excess. Refrigerate for 20 minutes. Line the tin with baking paper and spread a layer of baking beads or uncooked rice evenly over the paper. Bake for 15 minutes, remove the paper and beads and bake for another 15 minutes, or until golden.

To make the filling, put the egg yolks, sugar and cornflour in a bowl and whisk until pale. Heat the milk in a small saucepan until almost boiling, then remove from the heat and add gradually to the egg mixture, beating constantly. Strain into the pan. Stir constantly over low heat for 3 minutes, or until the mixture boils and thickens. Remove from the heat and add the vanilla extract. Transfer to a bowl, cover with plastic wrap and set aside to cool.

Spread the filling in the pastry shell and top with the berries. Melt the apricot jam over a low heat. Brush a thin layer over the fruit with a pastry brush and allow to set before cutting.

NOTE: In place of the jam, you can use baby apple gel. This will give a light, low-flavoured gloss to the finished tart.

Jalousie

SERVES 4–6

PREPARATION TIME: 40 MINUTES

COOKING TIME: 45 MINUTES

30 g (1 oz) unsalted butter
50 g (1¾ oz/¼ cup) soft brown sugar
500 g (1 lb 2 oz) apples, peeled, cored
    and cubed
1 teaspoon grated lemon zest
1 tablespoon lemon juice
¼ teaspoon freshly grated nutmeg
¼ teaspoon cinnamon
30 g (1 oz/¼ cup) sultanas
    (golden raisins)
375 g (13 oz) block ready-made puff
    pastry, thawed
1 egg, lightly beaten, to glaze

Preheat the oven to 220°C (425°F/Gas 7). Lightly grease a baking tray and line with baking paper.

Melt the butter and sugar in a frying pan. Add the apple, lemon zest and lemon juice. Cook over medium heat for 10 minutes, stirring occasionally, until the apples are cooked and the mixture is thick and syrupy. Stir in the nutmeg, cinnamon and sultanas. Cool completely.

Cut the block of puff pastry in half. On a lightly floured surface roll out one half of the pastry to an 18 x 24 cm (7 x 9½ inch) rectangle. Spread the fruit mixture onto the pastry, leaving a 2.5 cm (1 inch) border. Brush the edges lightly with the beaten egg.

Roll out the second half of pastry on a lightly floured surface to an 18 x 25 cm (7 x 10 inch) rectangle. Using a sharp knife, cut slashes in the pastry across its width, leaving a 2 cm (¾ inch) border around the edge. The slashes should open slightly and look like a venetian blind (jalousie in French). Place over the fruit and press the edges together. Trim away any extra pastry. Knock up the puff pastry (brush the sides upwards) with a knife to ensure rising during cooking. Glaze the top with egg. Bake for 25–30 minutes, or until puffed and golden.

Profiteroles with Dark Chocolate Sauce

🔺 SERVES 4–6
🔺 PREPARATION TIME: 40 MINUTES + COOLING
🔺 COOKING TIME: 50 MINUTES

60 g (2¼ oz) butter, chopped
90 g (3¼ oz/¾ cup) plain (all-purpose)
    flour
3 eggs, lightly beaten

WHITE CHOCOLATE FILLING
30 g (1 oz/¼ cup) custard powder
    or instant vanilla pudding mix
1 tablespoon caster (superfine) sugar
375 ml (13 fl oz/1½ cups) milk
150 g (5½ oz) white chocolate melts
    (buttons), chopped
1 tablespoon Grand Marnier

DARK CHOCOLATE SAUCE
125 g (4½ oz) dark chocolate, chopped
125 ml (4 fl oz/½ cup) cream

Preheat the oven to 210°C (415°F/Gas 6–7). Line a baking tray with baking paper. Put the butter and 185 ml (6 fl oz/¾ cup) water in a saucepan. Bring to the boil, then remove from the heat. Add the flour all at once. Return to the heat and stir until the mixture forms a smooth ball. Set aside to cool slightly. Transfer to a bowl and, while beating with electric beaters, gradually add the eggs a little at a time, beating well after each addition, to form a thick, smooth, glossy paste.

Spoon 2 heaped teaspoons of the mixture onto the tray at 5 cm (2 inch) intervals. Sprinkle lightly with water and bake for 12–15 minutes, or until the dough is puffed. Turn off the oven. Pierce a small hole in the base of each profiterole with the point of a knife and return the profiteroles to the oven. Leave them to dry in the oven for 5 minutes.

To make the filling, combine the custard powder or pudding mix and sugar in a saucepan. Gradually add the milk, stirring until smooth, then continue to stir over low heat until the mixture boils and thickens. Remove from the heat and add the white chocolate and Grand Marnier. Stir until the chocolate is melted. Cover the surface with plastic wrap and allow to cool. Stir the custard until smooth, then spoon into a piping bag fitted with a 1 cm (½ inch) plain nozzle. Pipe the filling into each profiterole.

To make the dark chocolate sauce, combine the chocolate and cream in a small saucepan. Stir over low heat until the chocolate is melted and the mixture is smooth. Serve warm with the filled profiteroles.

NOTE: The profiteroles can be made a day ahead. Fill just before serving. You can also make miniature profiteroles, using 1 teaspoon of the mixture. Dip the tops of the cooked profiteroles in melted chocolate. When set, fill them with whipped cream.

Date and Mascarpone Tart

🔺 SERVES 6–8

🔺 PREPARATION TIME: 50 MINUTES +

🔺 COOKING TIME: 45 MINUTES

COCONUT PASTRY

90 g (3¼ oz/½ cup) rice flour

60 g (2¼ oz/½ cup) plain (all-purpose) flour

100 g (3½ oz) unsalted butter, chilled and chopped

2 tablespoons icing (confectioners') sugar

25 g (1 oz/¼ cup) desiccated coconut

100 g (3½ oz) marzipan, grated

FILLING

8 fresh dates (about 200 g/7 oz), stoned and quartered, lengthways

2 eggs

2 teaspoons custard powder or instant vanilla pudding mix

125 g (4½ oz) mascarpone cheese

2 tablespoons caster (superfine) sugar

80 ml (2½ fl oz/⅓ cup) whipping cream

2 tablespoons flaked almonds

Preheat the oven to 180°C (350°F/Gas 4). Grease a shallow, 10 x 34 cm (4 x 13½ inch) fluted loose-based flan (tart) tin. Sift the flours into a large bowl. Using your fingertips, rub in the butter until the mixture resembles fine breadcrumbs, then press the mixture together gently. Stir in the icing sugar, coconut and marzipan. Turn out onto a lightly floured work surface and gather together into a ball. Flatten slightly, cover with plastic wrap and refrigerate for 15 minutes.

Roll out the pastry between two sheets of baking paper until large enough to line the tin. Ease the pastry into the tin and trim the edge. Refrigerate for 5–10 minutes. Line the pastry-lined tin with baking paper and spread a layer of baking beads or uncooked rice evenly over the paper. Place the tin on a baking tray and bake for 10 minutes. Remove the paper and beads and bake for another 5 minutes, or until just golden, then allow to cool.

Arrange the date quarters over the pastry. Whisk together the eggs, custard powder or pudding mix, mascarpone, caster sugar and cream until smooth. Pour the mixture over the dates, then sprinkle with the flaked almonds. Bake for 25–30 minutes, or until golden and just set, then allow to cool slightly. Serve warm.

Cherry Cheese Strudel

🔺 SERVES 8–10
🔺 PREPARATION TIME: 25 MINUTES
🔺 COOKING TIME: 45 MINUTES

500 g (1 lb 2 oz) ricotta cheese
2 teaspoons grated lemon or orange zest
55 g (2 oz/¼ cup) sugar
40 g (1½ oz/½ cup) fresh white
    breadcrumbs
2 tablespoons ground almonds
2 eggs
425 g (15 oz) tinned pitted black cherries
2 teaspoons cornflour (cornstarch)
8 sheets filo pastry
60 g (2¼ oz) unsalted butter, melted
2 tablespoons dry white breadcrumbs
icing (confectioners') sugar, for dusting

Preheat the oven to 180°C (350°F/Gas 4). Lightly grease a baking tray.

Combine the ricotta, zest, sugar, fresh breadcrumbs and almonds in a bowl. Add the eggs and mix well. Drain the cherries, reserving half the juice. Blend the cornflour with the reserved cherry juice in a saucepan. Stir over medium heat until the mixture boils and thickens, then cool slightly.

Layer the pastry sheets, brushing between each sheet with melted butter and sprinkling with a few dry breadcrumbs. Form a large square by placing the second sheet halfway down the first sheet. Alternate layers, brushing with melted butter and sprinkling with breadcrumbs.

Put the ricotta mixture along one long edge of the pastry. Shape into a log and top with cherries and cooled syrup. Roll the pastry around the ricotta filling, folding in the edges as you roll. Finish with a pastry edge underneath. Place on the prepared tray and bake for 35–40 minutes, or until the pastry is golden. Dust with icing sugar. Serve cold, cut into slices.

Banoffie Pie

🔺 SERVES 8

🔺 PREPARATION TIME: 35 MINUTES +

🔺 COOKING TIME: 30 MINUTES

WALNUT PASTRY

150 g (5½ oz/1¼ cups) plain
(all-purpose) flour

2 tablespoons icing (confectioners') sugar

85 g (3 oz/¾ cup) ground walnuts

80 g (2¾ oz) chilled unsalted butter,
chopped

FILLING

400 g (14 oz) tinned condensed milk

30 g (1 oz) unsalted butter

1 tablespoon golden syrup or dark
corn syrup

4 bananas, sliced

375 ml (13 fl oz/1½ cups) whipping
cream

50 g (1¾ oz) dark chocolate, melted

To make the walnut pastry, sift the flour and icing sugar into a large bowl and add the walnuts. Using your fingertips, rub in the butter until the mixture resembles fine breadcrumbs. Mix in 2–3 tablespoons of iced water with a flat-bladed knife, using a cutting action, until the mixture forms a firm dough. Add more water if the dough is too dry. Turn onto a lightly floured work surface and gather together into a ball. Wrap in plastic wrap and refrigerate for 15 minutes. Roll out to fit a 23 cm (9 inch) flan (tart) tin. Refrigerate for 20 minutes.

Preheat the oven to 180°C (350°F/Gas 4). Line the pastry base with baking paper and spread baking beads or uncooked rice over the paper. Bake for 15 minutes, remove the paper and beads and bake for another 10 minutes, or until lightly golden. Set aside to cool completely.

To make the filling, put the condensed milk, butter and golden syrup in a small saucepan. Stir over medium heat for 5 minutes, or until the mixture boils and thickens and turns a light caramel colour. Cool slightly, then arrange half the bananas over the pastry and pour the caramel over the top. Smooth the surface and refrigerate for 30 minutes.

Whip the cream, then drop spoonfuls of it over the caramel and arrange the remaining banana slices on top. Drizzle with melted chocolate.

Free-Form Blueberry Pie

🔺 SERVES 4

🔺 PREPARATION TIME: 20 MINUTES +

🔺 COOKING TIME: 35 MINUTES

185 g (6½ oz/1½ cups) plain
   (all-purpose) flour
60 g (2¼ oz/½ cup) icing
   (confectioners') sugar
125 g (4½ oz) chilled unsalted butter,
   cubed
60 ml (2 fl oz/¼ cup) lemon juice
500 g (1 lb 2 oz/2¼ cups) blueberries
30 g (1 oz/¼ cup) icing (confectioners')
   sugar, extra
1 teaspoon finely grated lemon zest
½ teaspoon ground cinnamon
1 egg white, lightly beaten
icing (confectioners') sugar, extra, to dust
whipped cream or ice cream, to serve

Preheat the oven to 180°C (350°F/Gas 4). Sift flour and icing sugar into a bowl. Using your fingertips, rub in the butter until the mixture resembles fine breadcrumbs. Make a well in the centre and add almost all the lemon juice. Mix together with a flat-bladed knife, using a cutting action, until the mixture comes together in beads. Add the remaining juice if the dough is too dry.

Gently gather the dough together and lift onto a sheet of baking paper. Roll out to a circle about 30 cm (12 inches) in diameter. Cover with plastic wrap and refrigerate for 10 minutes. Put the blueberries in a bowl and sprinkle them with the icing sugar, lemon zest and cinnamon.

Place the pastry (still on the baking paper) on a baking tray. Brush the centre of the pastry lightly with egg white. Pile the blueberry mixture onto the pastry in a 20 cm (8 inch) diameter circle, then fold the edges of the pastry over the filling, leaving the centre uncovered. Bake for 30–35 minutes. Dust with icing sugar and serve warm with whipped cream or ice cream.

Plum Tart

🔺 SERVES 6

🔺 PREPARATION TIME: 20 MINUTES

🔺 COOKING TIME: 35 MINUTES

500 g (1 lb 2 oz) block ready-made puff
   pastry, thawed

TOPPING
1 tablespoon plum jam
5 large plums, very thinly sliced
1 tablespoon brandy
1 tablespoon sugar

Preheat the oven to 200°C (400°F/Gas 6). Roll out the pastry on a lightly floured work surface to make an irregular rectangular shape, about 20 x 30 cm (8 x 12 inches) and 5 mm (¼ inch) thick. Place the pastry on a greased baking tray.

Heat the plum jam with 2 teaspoons water in a small saucepan over low heat until the jam is softened and spreadable. Brush the jam over the pastry base, leaving a 2 cm (¾ inch) border. Lay the plum slices along the pastry, leaving a 2 cm (¾ inch) border all around. Lightly brush the fruit with the brandy and sprinkle with the sugar. Bake for 30 minutes, or until the pastry is puffed and golden. Cut into slices and serve warm with cream or ice cream.

Free-Form Blueberry Pie

Linzertorte

🔺 SERVES 6–8
🔺 PREPARATION TIME: 30 MINUTES +
🔺 COOKING TIME: 30 MINUTES

100 g (3½ oz/⅔ cup) blanched almonds
185 g (6½ oz/1½ cups) plain
   (all-purpose) flour
½ teaspoon ground cinnamon
90 g (3¼ oz) unsalted butter, chilled and
   cubed
55 g (2 oz/¼ cup) caster (superfine)
   sugar
1 egg yolk
2–3 tablespoons lemon juice or water
320 g (11¼ oz/1 cup) raspberry jam
1 egg yolk, extra, to glaze
80 g (2¾ oz/¼ cup) apricot jam

Grind the almonds in a food processor until they are the consistency of medium coarse meal. Put the flour and cinnamon in a bowl. Using your fingertips, rub in the butter until the mixture resembles fine breadcrumbs. Stir in the caster sugar and almonds. Make a well in the centre and add the egg yolk and lemon juice. Mix with a flat-bladed knife, using a cutting action, until the mixture comes together in beads. Turn onto a lightly floured work surface and knead briefly until smooth. Wrap in plastic wrap and refrigerate for at least 20 minutes, to firm.

Roll two-thirds of the pastry out between two sheets of baking paper into a circle to fit a 20 cm (8 inch) round, loose-based, fluted flan (tart) tin. Press into the tin and trim away any excess pastry. Spread the raspberry jam over the base.

Roll out the remaining pastry, including any scraps, to a thickness of 3 mm (⅛ inch). Cut it into 2 cm (¾ inch) wide strips with a fluted cutter. Lay half the strips on a sheet of baking paper, leaving a 1 cm (½ inch) gap between each strip. Interweave the remaining strips to form a lattice pattern. Invert the lattice on top of the tart, remove the paper and trim the edge with a sharp knife. Cover with plastic wrap and refrigerate for 20 minutes.

Preheat the oven to 180°C (350°F/Gas 4). Place a baking tray in the oven to heat. Combine the extra egg yolk with 1 teaspoon water and brush over the tart. Place the tin on the heated tray and bake for 25–30 minutes, or until the pastry is golden brown.

Meanwhile, heat the apricot jam with 1 tablespoon of water, then strain the jam and brush over the tart while hot. Leave to cool in the tin, then remove and cut into wedges.

NOTE: Fluted cutters or special lattice cutters are available from speciality kitchenware stores. If you cannot obtain these, simply cut straight lines instead.

Lemon Brûlée Tarts

🌲 SERVES 4

🌲 PREPARATION TIME: 40 MINUTES +

🌲 COOKING TIME: 35 MINUTES

310 ml (10¾ fl oz/1¼ cups) cream

2 teaspoons grated lemon zest

4 egg yolks

2 tablespoons caster (superfine) sugar

2 teaspoons cornflour (cornstarch)

2 tablespoons lemon juice

410 g (14½ oz) block ready-made puff
  pastry, thawed or 2 sheets ready-rolled

80 g (2¾ oz/⅓ cup) sugar

Heat the cream in a saucepan with the lemon zest until almost boiling. Allow to cool slightly. Whisk the egg yolks, sugar, cornflour and lemon juice in a bowl until thick and pale.

Add the cream gradually, whisking constantly. Strain into a clean saucepan and stir over low heat until thickened slightly — the mixture should coat the back of a wooden spoon. Pour into a heatproof bowl, cover with plastic wrap and refrigerate for several hours or overnight.

Preheat the oven to 210°C (415°F/Gas 6–7). Lightly grease four 12 cm (4½ inch) shallow loose-based flan (tart) tins. If using block pastry, roll it to 25 x 48 cm (10 x 19 inches), then cut four rounds, large enough to fit the base and side of the tins. If using sheets, cut two rounds of pastry from each sheet to line the tins. Line each tin with pastry, trim the edges and prick the bases lightly with a fork. Line with baking paper and spread a layer of baking beads or uncooked rice evenly over the paper. Bake for 15 minutes, remove the paper and beads and bake for another 5 minutes, or until lightly golden. Leave to cool.

Spoon the lemon custard into each pastry shell, smooth the top, leaving a little room for the sugar layer. Cover the edges of the pastry with foil and sprinkle sugar generously over the surface of the custard in an even layer. Cook under a preheated grill (broiler) until the sugar just begins to colour. Put the tarts close to the grill so they brown quickly, but watch carefully that they do not burn. Serve immediately.

Tourte de Blettes

⟁ SERVES 6–8

⟁ PREPARATION TIME: 30 MINUTES +

⟁ COOKING TIME: 50 MINUTES

60 g (2¼ oz/½ cup) sultanas
  (golden raisins)
2 tablespoons brandy
400 g (14 oz) plain (all-purpose) flour
100 g (3½ oz) icing (confectioners') sugar
250 g (9 oz) unsalted butter, softened
  and chopped
3 eggs
800 g (1 lb 12 oz) silverbeet (Swiss
  chard), stalks removed
100 g (3½ oz/⅔ cup) pine nuts, toasted
  (see Note)
3 green cooking apples
1 teaspoon grated lemon zest
115 g (4 oz) mild goat's cheese, crumbled
1 egg yolk, to glaze
icing (confectioners') sugar, extra, to dust

Soak the sultanas in the brandy.

To make the pastry, sift the flour and 1 tablespoon of the icing sugar into a large bowl. Using your fingertips, rub in the butter until the mixture resembles fine breadcrumbs. Make a well in the centre, add one egg and mix with a flat-bladed knife, using a cutting action, until the mixture comes together in beads. Add 1 tablespoon water if the mixture is too dry. Gather together and lift onto a lightly floured work surface. Press into a ball and flatten to a disc. Wrap in plastic wrap and refrigerate for 30 minutes.

Preheat the oven to 180°C (350°F/Gas 4). Heat a baking tray in the oven.

Wash the silverbeet and pat dry. Place in a food processor with the two remaining eggs and the remaining icing sugar. Process to chop the silverbeet and combine, but don't overprocess. Transfer to a bowl. Drain the sultanas and add to the bowl with the pine nuts, then season.

Bring the pastry to room temperature, then break into two portions. Roll one half and use to line a 26 cm (10½ inch) loose-based flan (tart) tin.

Peel and core the apples, slice thinly. Toss the apples with the lemon zest. Put the silverbeet mixture on the pastry and top with the crumbled goat's cheese. Spiral the apple slices on top, making one or two layers.

Roll out the remaining pastry and cover the pie. Trim off the excess pastry and seal the edges with a little water. Crimp the edges.

Brush the pie with the egg yolk and bake for 45–50 minutes, or until golden. Cool and dust with icing sugar.

NOTE: To toast pine nuts, dry-fry them in a frying pan, stirring and watching them constantly so they don't burn.

Rhubarb Lattice Pie

⚘ SERVES 4–6

⚘ PREPARATION TIME: 35 MINUTES +

⚘ COOKING TIME: 1 HOUR

RHUBARB FILLING

500 g (1 lb 2 oz) rhubarb, trimmed,
  leaves discarded
115 g (4 oz/$^1/_2$ cup) caster (superfine)
  sugar
5 cm (2 inch) piece orange zest, pith
  removed
1 tablespoon orange juice
410 g (14$^1/_2$ oz) tinned pie apples
caster (superfine) sugar, extra, to taste

150 g (5$^1/_2$ oz/1$^1/_4$ cups) plain
  (all-purpose) flour
$^1/_4$ teaspoon baking powder
90 g (3$^1/_4$ oz) unsalted butter, chilled and
  cubed
1 tablespoon caster (superfine) sugar
80–100 ml (2$^1/_2$–3$^1/_2$ fl oz) iced water
milk, to glaze
raw (demerara) sugar, to decorate

To make the rhubarb filling, preheat the oven to 180°C (350°F/Gas 4). Cut the rhubarb into 3 cm (1$^1/_4$ inch) lengths and combine in a large casserole dish with the sugar, orange zest and juice. Cover the dish with a lid or foil and bake for 30 minutes, or until the rhubarb is just tender. Drain away any excess juice and discard the zest. Cool, then stir in the apple. Add more sugar to taste.

While the rhubarb is cooking, sift the flour and baking powder into a bowl. Using your fingertips, rub in the butter until the mixture resembles fine breadcrumbs. Stir in the sugar. Make a well in the centre and add almost all the water. Mix with a flat-bladed knife, using a cutting action, until the mixture comes together in beads. Add more water if the dough is too dry. Gather together, wrap in plastic wrap and chill for 20 minutes.

Roll the pastry out between two sheets of baking paper to a 28 cm (11$^1/_4$ inch) circle. Cut the pastry into 1.5 cm ($^5/_8$ inch) wide strips, using a sharp knife or a fluted cutter. Lay half the strips on a sheet of baking paper, leaving a 1 cm ($^1/_2$ inch) gap between each strip. Interweave the remaining strips to form a lattice. Cover with plastic wrap and refrigerate, flat, for 20 minutes.

Increase the oven to 210°C (415°F/Gas 6–7). Pour the filling into a 20 cm (8 inch) pie dish and smooth the surface. Invert the pastry lattice over the pie, remove the paper and trim the pastry edge. Bake for 10 minutes. Remove from the oven, brush with milk and sprinkle with sugar. Reduce the oven to 180°C (350°F/Gas 4) and bake the pie for 20 minutes, or until the pastry is golden and the filling is bubbling.

Almond Filo Snake

70 g ($2^1/_2$ oz/$^2/_3$ cup) ground almonds
30 g (1 oz/$^1/_3$ cup) flaked almonds
175 g (6 oz) icing (confectioners') sugar
1 egg, separated
1 teaspoon finely grated lemon zest
$^1/_4$ teaspoon natural almond extract
1 tablespoon rosewater
2 tablespoons olive oil
2 tablespoons almond oil
9 sheets filo pastry
pinch ground cinnamon
icing (confectioners') sugar, extra, to dust

Preheat the oven to 180°C (350°F/Gas 4). Lightly grease a 20 cm (8 inch) round spring-form tin.

Put all of the almonds in a bowl with the icing sugar. Put the egg white in a bowl and lightly beat with a fork. Add to the almonds with the lemon zest, almond extract and rosewater. Mix to a paste.

Divide the mixture into three and roll each portion into a sausage shape, 45 cm ($17^3/_4$ inches) long and 1 cm ($^1/_2$ inch) thick. If the paste is too sticky to roll, dust the bench with icing sugar.

Mix the oils in a bowl. Remove one sheet of filo and cover the rest with a damp tea towel (dish towel) to prevent them from drying out. Brush the filo sheet with the oils, then cover with two more oiled sheets. Place one almond 'sausage' along the length of the oiled pastry and roll up to enclose the filling. Form into a coil and sit the coil in the centre of the tin. Use oil to join the other sausages at their ends and continue shaping to make a large coil.

Add the cinnamon to the egg yolk and brush over the snake. Bake for 30 minutes, then remove the side of the tin and turn the snake over. Bake for another 10 minutes to crisp the base. Dust with icing sugar and serve warm.

NOTE: The snake will keep for up to 3 days but should not be refrigerated.

Treacle Tart

🔺 SERVES 4–6
🔺 PREPARATION TIME: 30 MINUTES +
🔺 COOKING TIME: 35 MINUTES

SHORTCRUST PASTRY
150 g (5½ oz/1¼ cups) plain
    (all-purpose) flour
90 g (3¼ oz) chilled unsalted butter,
    chopped
2–3 tablespoons iced water
1 egg, lightly beaten, to glaze

FILLING
350 g (12 oz/1 cup) golden syrup
    or dark corn syrup
25 g (1 oz) unsalted butter
½ teaspoon ground ginger
140 g (5 oz/1¾ cups) fresh white
    breadcrumbs

icing (confectioners') sugar, to dust
    (optional)

To make the pastry, sift the flour into a large bowl. Using your fingertips, rub in the butter until the mixture resembles fine breadcrumbs. Add almost all the iced water and mix to a firm dough with a flat-bladed knife, using a cutting action. Add more water if the dough is too dry. Turn onto a lightly floured work surface and gather together into a ball. Cover with plastic wrap and refrigerate for 20 minutes.

Brush a 20 cm (8 inch) flan (tart) tin with melted butter or oil. Roll out the pastry large enough to fit the base and side of the tin, allowing a 4 cm (1½ inch) overhang. Ease the pastry into the tin and trim by running a rolling pin firmly across the top of the tin. Re-roll the trimmed pastry to a rectangle 10 x 20 cm (4 x 8 inches). Using a sharp knife or fluted pastry wheel, cut into long 1 cm (½ inch) wide strips. Cover the pastry-lined tin and strips with plastic wrap and refrigerate for 20 minutes. Preheat the oven to 180°C (350°F/Gas 4).

To make the filling, combine the golden syrup, butter and ginger in a small saucepan and stir over low heat until the butter melts. Stir in the breadcrumbs until combined. Pour the mixture into the pastry case. Lay half the pastry strips over the tart, starting at the centre and working outwards. Lay the remaining strips over the tart to form a lattice pattern. Brush the lattice with beaten egg. Bake for 30 minutes, or until the pastry is lightly golden. Serve warm or at room temperature. You can dust the top with icing sugar and serve with ice cream or cream.

Apple Pie

🌲 SERVES 6
🌲 PREPARATION TIME: 45 MINUTES +
🌲 COOKING TIME: 50 MINUTES

FILLING
6 large granny smith apples, peeled,
    cored and cut into wedges
2 tablespoons caster (superfine) sugar
1 teaspoon finely grated lemon zest
pinch ground cloves

PASTRY
250 g (9 oz/2 cups) plain (all-purpose)
    flour
30 g (1 oz/¼ cup) self-raising flour
150 g (5½ oz) unsalted butter, chilled
    and cubed
2 tablespoons caster (superfine) sugar
80–100 ml (2½–3½ fl oz) iced water
2 tablespoons marmalade
1 egg, lightly beaten
1 tablespoon sugar

Lightly grease a 23 cm (9 inch) pie dish.

To make the filling, put the apple in a saucepan with the sugar, lemon zest, cloves and 2 tablespoons water. Cover and cook over low heat for 8 minutes, or until the apples are just tender, shaking the pan occasionally. Drain and cool completely.

To make the pastry, sift the flours into a bowl. Using your fingertips, rub in the butter until the mixture resembles fine breadcrumbs. Stir in the sugar, then make a well in the centre. Add almost all the iced water and mix with a flat-bladed knife, using a cutting action, until the mixture comes together in beads. Add more water if the dough is too dry. Gather together and lift out onto a lightly floured work surface. Press into a ball and divide into two, making one piece a little bigger. Cover with plastic wrap and refrigerate for 20 minutes.

Preheat the oven to 200°C (400°F/Gas 6). Roll out the larger piece of pastry between two sheets of baking paper to line the base and side of the pie dish. Line the pie dish with the pastry. Use a small sharp knife to trim away any excess pastry. Brush the marmalade over the base and spoon the apple mixture into the shell. Roll out the other pastry between the baking paper until large enough to cover the pie. Brush water around the rim then lay the pastry top over the pie. Trim off any excess pastry, pinch the edges and cut a few slits in the top to allow steam to escape.

Re-roll the pastry trimmings and cut into leaves for decoration. Lightly brush the top with egg, then sprinkle with sugar. Bake for 20 minutes, then reduce the oven temperature to 180°C (350°F/Gas 4) and bake for another 15–20 minutes, or until golden.

Banana Tart

🌲 SERVES 6
🌲 PREPARATION TIME: 40 MINUTES +
🌲 COOKING TIME: 35 MINUTES

FLAKY PASTRY
220 g (7¾ oz/1¾ cups) plain
    (all-purpose) flour
60 g (2¼ oz) unsalted butter
150 ml (5 fl oz) iced water
100 g (3½ oz) unsalted butter, extra,
    chilled

zest and juice of 2 oranges
80 g (2¾ oz/⅓ cup) soft brown sugar
¼ teaspoon cardamom seeds
1 tablespoon rum
3–4 ripe bananas

To make the pastry, sift the flour into a bowl with a pinch of salt. Using your fingertips, rub in the butter until the mixture resembles fine breadcrumbs. Add enough of the iced water, mixing with a flat-bladed knife and using a cutting action, to make a dough-like consistency. Turn onto a lightly floured work surface and knead until just smooth.

Roll into a rectangle 10 x 30 cm (4 x 12 inches), cut one-third of the extra chilled butter into cubes and dot all over the top two-thirds of the pastry, leaving a little room around the edge. Fold the bottom third of the pastry up and the top third down and press the edges down to seal. Now turn the pastry to your left, so the hinge is on your right, and roll and fold as before using another third of the butter. Refrigerate for 20 minutes, then with the hinge to your right, roll it out again, cover the top two-thirds of the pastry with another third of the butter and fold and roll. Repeat, using the rest of the butter and then fold and roll once more without adding any butter.

Roll the pastry out on a lightly floured work surface into a rectangle 25 x 30 cm (10 x 12 inches), cut a 2 cm (¾ inch) strip off each side and use this to make a frame on the pastry by brushing the edges of the pastry with water and sticking the strips onto it. Trim off any excess and put the tart base on a baking tray lined with baking paper, cover with plastic wrap and refrigerate until required.

Combine the orange zest, juice, brown sugar and cardamom seeds in a small saucepan, bring to the boil, simmer for 5 minutes, then remove from the heat and add the rum. Set aside to cool. Preheat the oven to 220°C (425°F/Gas 7).

Slice the bananas in half lengthways, arrange on the tart in an even layer, cut side up, and brush with a little of the rum syrup. Bake on the top shelf of the oven for 20–30 minutes, making sure the pastry does not overbrown. Brush with more syrup and serve.

Lime Chiffon Pie

🌿 SERVES 12

🌿 PREPARATION TIME: 30 MINUTES +

🌿 COOKING TIME: 1 HOUR

ALMOND PASTRY

150 g (5½ oz/1¼ cups) plain
  (all-purpose) flour
90 g (3¼ oz) ground almonds
90 g (3¼ oz) unsalted butter, chilled and
  chopped
1–2 tablespoons iced water

FILLING

6 egg yolks
115 g (4 oz/½ cup) caster (superfine)
  sugar
100 g (3½ oz) unsalted butter, melted
80 ml (2½ fl oz/⅓ cup) lime juice
2 teaspoons finely grated lime zest
2 teaspoons powdered gelatine
125 ml (4 fl oz/½ cup) whipping cream

110 g (3¾ oz/½ cup) sugar
zest of 4 limes, finely shredded

Sift the flour into a large bowl and add the almonds. Using your fingertips, rub in the butter until the mixture resembles fine breadcrumbs. Add almost all the iced water and mix with a flat-bladed knife, using a cutting action, until the mixture forms a firm dough. Add more water if necessary. Turn onto a lightly floured surface and gather together into a ball. Roll the pastry out to fit a 23 cm (9 inch) fluted flan (tart) tin. Line the tin, trim the edges and refrigerate for 20 minutes.

Preheat the oven to 180°C (350°F/Gas 4). Line the pastry-lined tin with a sheet of baking paper and spread a layer of baking beads or uncooked rice evenly over the paper. Bake for 20 minutes, then remove the paper and beads and bake for another 20 minutes, or until lightly golden. Allow to cool completely.

To make the filling, put the egg yolks, caster sugar, butter, lime juice and zest in a heatproof bowl. Whisk to combine thoroughly and dissolve the sugar. Stand the bowl over a saucepan of simmering water, making sure the base of the bowl does not touch the water, and stir constantly for 15 minutes, or until the mixture thickens. Remove from the heat and cool slightly. Put 1 tablespoon water in a small heatproof bowl, sprinkle the gelatine in an even layer over the surface and leave to go spongy. Do not stir. Bring a saucepan filled with about 4 cm (1½ inches) of water to the boil, remove from the heat and place the bowl into the pan. The water should come halfway up the side of the bowl. Stir the gelatine until clear and dissolved. Cool slightly, add to the lime curd and stir to combine. Cool to room temperature, stirring occasionally.

Whip the cream then fold through the lime curd and pour into the pastry case. Refrigerate for 2–3 hours to set. Leave for 15 minutes at room temperature before serving.

To make the lime zest, mix the sugar with 1 tablespoon water in a small saucepan. Stir over low heat until the sugar has dissolved. Bring to the boil, add the zest and simmer for 3 minutes. Drain the zest on a wire rack, then decorate the lime chiffon pie before serving.

Apple Strudel

⚶ MAKES 2 STRUDELS

⚶ PREPARATION TIME: 20 MINUTES

⚶ COOKING TIME: 30 MINUTES

30 g (1 oz) unsalted butter

4 green cooking apples, peeled, cored
    and thinly sliced

2 tablespoons orange juice

1 tablespoon honey

55 g (2 oz/¼ cup) sugar

60 g (2¼ oz/½ cup) sultanas
    (golden raisins)

2 sheets ready-rolled puff pastry, thawed

25 g (1 oz/¼ cup) ground almonds

1 egg, lightly beaten

2 tablespoons soft brown sugar

1 teaspoon ground cinnamon

Preheat the oven to 220°C (425°F/Gas 7). Brush two baking trays lightly with melted butter or oil. Heat the butter in a saucepan. Add the apple slices and cook for 2 minutes until lightly golden. Add the orange juice, honey, sugar and sultanas. Stir over medium heat until the sugar dissolves and the apple is just tender. Transfer the mixture to a bowl and leave until completely cooled.

Place one sheet of pastry on a flat work surface. Fold it in half and make small cuts in the folded edge of the pastry at 2 cm (¾ inch) intervals. Open out the pastry and sprinkle with half of the ground almonds. Drain away the liquid from the apple and place half of the mixture in the centre of the pastry. Brush the edges with some of the lightly beaten egg, and fold over, pressing firmly to seal.

Place the strudel on a baking tray, seam-side down. Brush the top with egg and sprinkle with half of the combined brown sugar and cinnamon. Repeat the process with the other sheet of pastry, remaining filling and the rest of the brown sugar and cinnamon. Bake for 20–25 minutes, or until the pastry is golden and crisp. Serve hot with cream or ice cream, or at room temperature as a teatime treat.

Passionfruit Tart

🌿 SERVES 8

🌿 PREPARATION TIME: 30 MINUTES +

🌿 COOKING TIME: 1 HOUR

90 g (3¼ oz/¾ cup) plain (all-purpose)
   flour
2 tablespoons icing (confectioners') sugar
2 tablespoons custard powder or instant
   vanilla pudding mix
30 g (1 oz) unsalted butter
60 ml (2 fl oz/¼ cup) light evaporated
   milk
icing (confectioners') sugar, extra, to dust

FILLING
pulp from about 8 passionfruit
125 g (4½ oz/½ cup) ricotta cheese
1 teaspoon natural vanilla extract
30 g (1 oz/¼ cup) icing (confectioners')
   sugar
2 eggs, lightly beaten
185 ml (6 fl oz/¾ cup) light evaporated
   milk

Preheat the oven to 200°C (400°F/Gas 6). Lightly spray a 23 cm (9 inch) loose-based flan (tart) tin with oil spray. Sift the flour, icing sugar and custard powder into a bowl. Using your fingertips, rub in the butter until the mixture resembles fine breadcrumbs. Add almost all the milk. Mix with a flat-bladed knife, using a cutting action, until the mixture forms a soft dough. Add more milk if the dough is too dry. Bring together on a lightly floured work surface until just smooth. Form into a ball, wrap in plastic wrap and refrigerate for 15 minutes.

Roll the pastry out on a lightly floured surface, large enough to fit the tin, then refrigerate for 15 minutes. Cover with baking paper and spread evenly with baking beads or uncooked rice. Bake for 10 minutes, remove the paper and beads and bake for another 5–8 minutes, or until golden. Cool. Reduce the oven to 160°C (315°F/Gas 2–3).

Strain the passionfruit pulp to remove the seeds, reserving 2 teaspoons of seeds. Beat the ricotta with the vanilla extract and icing sugar until smooth. Add the eggs and passionfruit pulp, reserved seeds and milk, then beat well. Put the tin on a baking tray and gently pour in the mixture. Bake for 40 minutes, or until set. Cool in the tin. Dust the edges with icing sugar just before serving.

Rice Tart

🌿 SERVES 8–10

🌿 PREPARATION TIME: 25 MINUTES +

🌿 COOKING TIME: 1 HOUR 35 MINUTES

PASTRY

155 g (5½ oz/1¼ cups) plain
　(all-purpose) flour

55 g (2¼ oz/¼ cup) caster (superfine)
　sugar

125 g (4½ oz) unsalted butter, chilled and
　cubed

2 egg yolks

1 teaspoon natural vanilla extract

FILLING

60 g (2¼ oz/½ cup) raisins

2 tablespoons cognac or brandy

110 g (3¾ oz/½ cup) risotto rice

750 ml (26 fl oz/3 cups) cream

1 vanilla bean, split

2 cinnamon sticks

6 egg yolks

180 g (6½ oz/¾ cup) caster (superfine)
　sugar

50 g (1¾ oz/⅓ cup) pine nuts, toasted

1½ teaspoons finely grated lemon zest

lightly whipped cream, to serve

To make the pastry, sift the flour into a bowl and add the sugar and a pinch of salt. Add the butter and toss to coat in the flour mix. Rub the butter into the flour with your fingertips for about 5 minutes, or until it resembles fine breadcrumbs, then make a well in the centre.

Mix the egg yolks, vanilla and 60 ml (2 fl oz/¼ cup) cold water together, then pour into the well. Using a flat-bladed knife, cut into the mixture while you turn the bowl until it is well combined and comes together in small beads. Gather the dough together. Press into a ball. Flatten into a 2 cm (¾ inch) thick disc. Cover with plastic wrap and refrigerate for 30 minutes.

Roll the pastry out between two sheets of plastic wrap until it is 36 cm (14 inches) in diameter. Remove the top layer of baking paper and invert the pastry onto a 28 cm (11¼ inch) fluted tart dish. Remove the final layer of paper and press the pastry into the dish, allowing extra overhang on the sides, then trim the edges. Prick the base all over with a fork then refrigerate for 1 hour.

Preheat the oven to 180°C (350°F/Gas 4). Combine the raisins and cognac. Set aside to soak. Cook the rice in boiling water for 15 minutes, or until tender. Drain, rinse with cold water and leave to drain and cool. Place the cream, vanilla bean and cinnamon in a saucepan and bring almost to the boil over medium heat. Remove from the heat. Set aside to cool.

Remove the tart from the fridge, line with lightly crumpled baking paper and spread some baking beads or uncooked rice evenly over the base. Bake for 15 minutes then remove the paper and beads and cook for a further 10–15 minutes, or until lightly golden all over. Remove from the oven and set aside to cool. Reduce the temperature to 150°C (300°F/Gas 2).

Beat the egg yolks and sugar together until thick. Strain the cream mixture and stir into the eggs. Combine the rice with the raisins, pine nuts and lemon zest. Spread the rice mixture over the base of the tart shell, then pour over the custard. Bake for 45 minutes, or until just set.

Chocolate and Peanut Butter Pie

🔺 SERVES 10–12
🔺 PREPARATION TIME: 20 MINUTES
🔺 COOKING TIME: 10 MINUTES

200 g (7 oz) chocolate biscuits (cookies)
  with cream centre, crushed
50 g (1³/₄ oz) unsalted butter, melted
200 g (³/₄ cup) cream cheese
85 g (²/₃ cup) icing (confectioners')
  sugar, sifted
100 g (²/₃ cup) smooth peanut butter
1 teaspoon natural vanilla extract
250 ml (9 fl oz/1 cup) whipping cream
60 ml (2 fl oz/¹/₄ cup) cream, extra
3 teaspoons unsalted butter, extra
50 g (1³/₄ oz) dark chocolate, grated
honey-roasted peanuts, chopped,
  to garnish

Combine the biscuit crumbs with the melted butter and press into the base and side of a deep 23 x 18 x 3 cm (9 x 7 x 1¹/₄ inch) pie dish and refrigerate for 15 minutes, or until firm.

Put the cream cheese and icing sugar in a bowl and beat with electric beaters until smooth. Add the peanut butter and vanilla and beat together. Whip the cream, then add a third of it and stir until smooth, then gently fold in the remaining whipped cream. Pour the mixture into the pie shell. Refrigerate for 2 hours, or until firm.

Place the extra cream and butter in a pan and stir over medium heat until the butter is melted and the cream just comes to a simmer. Remove from the heat, add the grated chocolate, and stir until melted. Cool a little, then dribble the chocolate over the top of the pie to create a lattice pattern. Refrigerate for 2 hours, or until the topping and chocolate are firm.

Remove the pie from the fridge, scatter over the chopped peanuts and serve.

Feuilleté with Cherries Jubilee

SERVES 4

PREPARATION TIME: 15 MINUTES +

COOKING TIME: 25 MINUTES

375 g (13 oz) block ready-made puff
   pastry, thawed
1 egg, lightly beaten
20 g ($^3/_4$ oz) unsalted butter
20 g ($^3/_4$ oz) sugar
500 g (1 lb 2 oz) cherries, pitted
300 ml (10$^1/_2$ fl oz) thick (double/heavy)
   cream
125 ml (4 fl oz/$^1/_2$ cup) brandy or Kirsch
icing (confectioners') sugar, to dust

To make the feuilletés, roll the pastry out on a floured work surface and cut out four rectangles of 10 x 12 cm (4 x 4$^1/_2$ inches) each. Put them on a baking tray and brush with the beaten egg, being careful not to let any drip down the sides of the pastry. Refrigerate for 30 minutes. Preheat the oven to 220°C (425°F/Gas 7).

Melt the butter and sugar together in a saucepan and add the cherries. Cook over high heat for about 1 minute, then reduce the heat and simmer for about 3 minutes, or until the cherries are tender. Reduce the heat to low and keep the cherries warm.

Bake the feuilletés on the top shelf of the oven for 15 minutes until golden and puffed, then cut them in half horizontally and gently pull any doughy bits out of the centre. Turn the oven off and put the feuilletés back in the oven to dry out for a couple of minutes.

When you are ready to serve, whisk the cream until it reaches stiff peaks. Place a warm feuilleté base on each serving plate. Heat the brandy or Kirsch in a small saucepan and set it alight, then pour it over the cherries (keep a saucepan lid nearby in case the flames get too high). Spoon some cherries into each feuilleté and top with a little cream. Put the lids on and dust with icing sugar before serving.

Sicilian Cheesecake

🔺 SERVES 8

🔺 PREPARATION TIME: 45 MINUTES +

🔺 COOKING TIME: 1 HOUR 25 MINUTES

250 g (9 oz/2 cups) plain (all-purpose)
    flour
165 g (5¾ oz) unsalted butter, chopped
55 g (2¼ oz/¼ cup) caster (superfine)
    sugar
1 teaspoon grated lemon zest
1 egg, lightly beaten

FILLING
60 g (2¼ oz) raisins, chopped
80 ml (2½ fl oz/⅓ cup) Marsala
500 g (1 lb 2 oz/2 cups) ricotta cheese
115 g (4 oz/½ cup) caster (superfine)
    sugar
1 tablespoon plain (all-purpose) flour
4 eggs, separated
125 ml (4 fl oz/½ cup) cream

Lightly grease a 26 cm (10½ inch) spring-form cake tin. Sift the flour and a pinch of salt into a large bowl and rub in the butter, using just your fingertips. Add the sugar, lemon zest, egg and a little water, if necessary and, with a flat-bladed knife, use a cutting action until a rough dough forms. Gather the dough together into a ball.

Roll out the dough between two sheets of baking paper to fit the base and side of the tin, then chill for 30 minutes. Preheat the oven to 190°C (375°F/Gas 5). Prick the pastry base, line with baking paper and spread a layer of baking beads or uncooked rice over the pastry. Bake for 15 minutes, remove the paper and beads and bake for 8 minutes, or until the pastry is dry. If the base puffs up, gently press down with the back of a spoon. Allow to cool. Reduce the oven temperature to 160°C (315°F/Gas 2–3).

To make the filling, put the raisins and Marsala in a small bowl, cover and leave to soak. Push the ricotta through a sieve, then beat with the sugar, using a wooden spoon, until combined. Add the flour and egg yolks, then the cream and undrained raisins and mix well. In a clean, dry bowl, beat the egg whites until soft peaks form, then fold into the ricotta mixture in two batches.

Pour the filling into the pastry case and bake for 1 hour, or until just set. Check during cooking and cover with foil if the pastry is overbrowning. Cool a little in the oven with the door ajar to prevent sinking. Serve warm.

NOTE: Marsala is a fortified dark wine made in Sicily with a deep rich flavour. It is available in dry and sweet varieties. Sweet Marsala is used in desserts and as a dessert wine.

small bites

Custard Rolls

🔺 MAKES 18
🔺 PREPARATION TIME: 35 MINUTES
🔺 COOKING TIME: 20 MINUTES

375 ml (13 fl oz/1½ cups) milk
115 g (4 oz/½ cup) caster (superfine)
    sugar
60 g (2¼ oz/½ cup) semolina
1 teaspoon grated lemon zest
1 egg, lightly beaten
12 sheets filo pastry
125 g (4½ oz) unsalted butter, melted
2 tablespoons icing (confectioners') sugar
½ teaspoon ground cinnamon

Put the milk, caster sugar, semolina and lemon zest in a saucepan and stir until coming to the boil. Reduce the heat and simmer for 3 minutes.

Remove from the heat and gradually whisk in the egg. Pour the custard into a bowl, cover the surface with plastic wrap and set aside to cool. Preheat the oven to 180°C (350°F/Gas 4). Lightly brush two baking trays with melted butter.

Work with two sheets of pastry at a time. Cover the rest with a tea towel (dish towel). Brush one sheet with melted butter, then top with another. Cut lengthways into three strips. Brush the edges with melted butter.

Spoon about 1 tablespoon of the custard 5 cm (2 inches) in from the short edge of each pastry strip. Roll the pastry over the filling, fold the ends in, then roll up. Repeat with the remaining pastry and custard. Arrange on the trays 2 cm (¾ inch) apart. Brush with the remaining butter. Bake for 12–15 minutes, or until crisp and golden. Cool on a wire rack. Dust with a little of the combined icing sugar and cinnamon.

Sacher Squares

🔺 MAKES 24
🔺 PREPARATION TIME: 1 HOUR
🔺 COOKING TIME: 40 MINUTES

BASE
125 g (4½ oz/1 cup) plain (all-purpose)
    flour
60 g (2¼ oz) unsalted butter, chopped
60 g (2¼ oz/¼ cup) sugar
2 egg yolks, lightly beaten

CAKE
125 g (4½ oz/1 cup) plain (all-purpose)
    flour
40 g (1½ oz/⅓ cup) unsweetened cocoa
    powder
230 g (8 oz/1 cup) caster (superfine)
    sugar
100 g (3½ oz) unsalted butter
2 tablespoons apricot jam
4 eggs, separated
315 g (11 oz/1 cup) apricot jam, extra

TOPPING
250 g (9 oz/1⅔ cups) chopped dark
    chocolate
185 ml (6 fl oz/¾ cup) cream

Preheat the oven to 180°C (350°F/Gas 4). Cover a baking tray with baking paper. Lightly grease a shallow 18 x 28 cm (7 x 11¼ inch) cake tin and line the base and side with baking paper, extending over two sides.

To make the base, sift the flour into a large bowl and add the butter. Rub in until the mixture resembles fine breadcrumbs. Stir in the sugar and make a well in the centre. Add the egg yolks and 1½ teaspoons of iced water and mix with a flat-bladed knife, using a cutting action, to form a firm dough, adding more water if necessary. Gently gather the dough and lift onto a lightly floured surface. Roll out the pastry to 18 x 28 cm (7 x 11¼ inch) rectangle and bake on a baking tray for 10 minutes, or until just golden. Cool completely.

To make the cake, sift the flour and cocoa into a large bowl. Make a well in the centre. Combine the sugar, butter and jam in a small saucepan and stir over low heat until the butter has melted and the sugar has dissolved. Remove from the heat. Add the butter mixture to the dry ingredients and stir until just combined. Mix in the egg yolks. Beat the egg whites in a small bowl until soft peaks form. Using a metal spoon, fold the egg whites into the cake mixture. Pour into the tin and bake for 30 minutes, or until a skewer comes out clean. Leave in the tin for 15 minutes before turning out onto a wire rack to cool.

Warm the extra jam, then push through a fine sieve. Brush the pastry base with 3 tablespoons of the jam. Place the cake on the base. Trim the sides evenly. Using a serrated knife, cut into 24 squares. Brush the top and sides of each square with jam, and place each one on a large wire rack, over a piece of baking paper, spacing them 4 cm (1½ inches) apart.

To make the topping, put the chocolate in a small bowl. Put the cream in a small pan and bring to the boil. Remove from the heat, pour over the chocolate and leave for 5 minutes, then stir until the mixture is smooth. Cool slightly. Spoon the topping over each square. Spoon any left-over topping into a small piping (icing) bag and pipe an 'S' onto each square.

Egg Tarts

OUTER DOUGH
165 g (5¾ oz/1⅓ cups) plain
    (all-purpose) flour
2 tablespoons icing (confectioners') sugar
2 tablespoons oil

INNER DOUGH
125 g (4½ oz/1 cup) plain (all-purpose)
    flour
100 g (3½ oz) lard, chopped

CUSTARD
55 g (2 oz/¼ cup) caster (superfine)
    sugar
2 eggs

To make the outer dough, sift the flour and icing sugar into a bowl. Make a well in the centre. Combine the oil with 80 ml (2½ oz/⅓ cup) water and pour into the dry ingredients. Mix with a flat-bladed knife, using a cutting action, to form a rough dough. (If the flour is very dry, add a little water.) Turn out onto a lightly floured surface and gather into a smooth ball. Cover and set aside for 15 minutes. To make the inner dough, sift the flour into a bowl. Using your fingertips, rub the lard into the flour until the mixture resembles breadcrumbs. Press the dough into a ball, cover and set aside for 15 minutes.

On a lightly floured surface, roll the outer dough into a 10 x 20 cm (4 x 8 inch) rectangle. Roll the inner dough into a smaller rectangle, one-third the size of the outer dough. Place the inner dough in the centre of the outer dough. Fold the outer dough over the inner dough so the short edges overlap and the inner dough is enclosed. Pinch the edges together to seal. Roll the dough away from you in one direction into a long rectangle, until it is half as thick as it was previously. Fold the pastry into three layers by taking the left-hand third over first, and then folding the right-hand third on top. Wrap the dough in plastic wrap and refrigerate for 30 minutes. Preheat the oven to 210°C (415°F/Gas 6–7). Brush two 12-hole muffin tins with melted butter or oil.

To make the custard, put 80 ml (2½ oz/⅓ cup) water and the sugar in a saucepan and stir, without boiling, until the sugar dissolves. Bring to the boil and simmer, without stirring, for 1 minute. Cool for 5 minutes. Put the eggs in a bowl and beat lightly with a fork. Whisk the sugar syrup into the eggs until just combined. Strain.

Place the pastry on a lightly floured surface. With one open end towards you, roll the pastry out to a rectangle, 3 mm (⅛ inch) thick. Cut out rounds of pastry using a 7 cm (2¾ inch) fluted cutter and carefully place the rounds into the tins. Fill each pastry case two-thirds full with custard. Bake for 15 minutes, or until just set. Be careful not to overcook the custard. Leave to cool in the tins for 3 minutes, then remove and cool on a wire rack.

Amandine

🔺 SERVES 4–6
🔺 PREPARATION TIME: 25 MINUTES
🔺 COOKING TIME: 30 MINUTES

100 g (3½ oz) hazelnuts
120 g (4¼ oz) almonds
185 g (6½ oz/1 cup) soft brown sugar
360 g (12¾ oz/1⅔ cups) sugar
175 g (6 oz/½ cup) honey
1 lemon, halved
115 g (4 oz) unsalted butter

Preheat the oven to 170°C (325°F/Gas 3). Spread the hazelnuts on a baking tray and roast for about 5 minutes, or until their skins crack. Remove from the oven and reduce the temperature to 150°C (300°F/Gas 2). Wrap them in a tea towel (dish towel), rub together to dislodge their skins and allow to cool. Put the skinned nuts into a food processor. Place the almonds on the baking tray and bake for 6 minutes, or until browned. Allow to cool, then transfer the almonds to the processor. Chop the nuts until they look like little pebbles.

Grease a large baking tray. Place the sugars and honey with 125 ml (4 fl oz/½ cup) of water in a heavy-based saucepan. Bring to the boil, stirring only until the sugars have melted. Remove any seeds visible in the lemon halves and squeeze 2–3 drops of juice into the boiling syrup. Reserve the lemons. Simmer the syrup for 8–10 minutes, or until it reaches 150°C (300°F). Stir in the butter and, when melted, add the nuts. Pour onto the prepared surface and, using the lemon halves as tools, spread and smooth the toffee out to a 5 mm (¼ inch) thick sheet. Leave to cool and set. Crack into pieces for serving.

Sorbet Balls

🔺 MAKES 24
🔺 PREPARATION TIME: 20 MINUTES +
🔺 COOKING TIME: 5 MINUTES

400 g (14 oz) sorbet
250 g (9 oz/1²⁄₃ cups) dark chocolate
  melts (buttons)

Soften the sorbet slightly and spread it out in a shallow container to a depth of about 2.5 cm (1 inch). Put in the freezer until solid.

Cover a baking tray with baking paper and place in the freezer. Using a melon baller, scoop out tiny balls of sorbet and place them on the prepared tray. Put a cocktail stick in each sorbet ball. Cover the tray tightly with plastic wrap, ensuring it is completely covered so it doesn't dry out, then refreeze overnight so the balls are solid.

Place the chocolate in a heatproof bowl. Bring a saucepan of water to the boil, then remove the pan from the heat. Sit the bowl over the pan, making sure the base of the bowl doesn't touch the water. Stir occasionally until the chocolate has melted. Remove the bowl and set aside to cool a little.

Ladle some of the melted chocolate into a separate bowl so that if anything goes wrong you won't ruin the whole batch. Work with just a few balls at a time so they do not melt. Dip each sorbet ball in the chocolate, making sure it is thoroughly coated and place it back on the tray. Return to the freezer. Reheat the chocolate if necessary. It must be liquid enough not to coat too thickly. Add more melted chocolate to the bowl when necessary, but if it seizes, start with a new bowl and a new batch. Freeze until you are ready to serve. Serve these on a bed of crushed ice or pile them into an iced bowl.

NOTE: To make an ice bowl, fill a bowl half-full of water and float some flower petals and herb leaves in it. Place another bowl inside and weigh it down so it sits down in the water but does not sink to the bottom. The water should form a bowl-shaped layer between the two bowls. Freeze overnight. Separate the bowls by rubbing a cloth dipped in hot water over them and twisting them apart.

Vanilla Slice

🔺 PREPARATION TIME: 40 MINUTES
🔺 COOKING TIME: 15 MINUTES

500 g (1 lb 2 oz) block ready-made puff
   pastry, thawed
230 g (8½ oz/1 cup) caster (superfine)
   sugar
90 g (3¼ oz/¾ cup) cornflour
   (cornstarch)
60 g (2¼ oz/½ cup) custard powder
   or instant vanilla pudding mix
1 litre (35 fl oz/4 cups) cream
60 g (2¼ oz) unsalted butter, cubed
2 teaspoons natural vanilla extract
3 egg yolks

ICING
185 g (6½ oz/1½ cups) icing
   (confectioners') sugar
60 g (2¼ oz/¼ cup) passionfruit pulp
15 g (½ oz) unsalted butter, melted

Preheat the oven to 210°C (415°F/Gas 6–7). Grease two baking trays with oil. Line the base and sides of a shallow 23 cm (9 inch) square cake tin with foil, leaving the foil hanging over on two opposite sides. Divide the pastry in half, roll each piece to a 25 cm (10 inch) square about 3 mm (⅛ inch) thick and place each one on a prepared tray. Prick all over with a fork and bake for 8 minutes, or until golden. Trim each pastry sheet to a 23 cm (9 inch) square. Place one sheet, top side down, in the cake tin.

Combine the sugar, cornflour and custard powder in a saucepan. Gradually add the cream and stir until smooth. Place over medium heat and stir constantly for 2 minutes, or until the mixture boils and thickens. Add the butter and vanilla and stir until smooth. Remove from the heat and whisk in the egg yolks until combined. Spread the custard over the pastry in the tin and cover with the remaining pastry, top side down. Allow to cool.

To make the icing (frosting), combine the icing sugar, passionfruit pulp and butter in a small bowl and stir together until smooth.

Lift the slice out, using the foil as handles, spread the icing over the top and leave it to set before carefully cutting into squares with a serrated knife.

Shredded Pastries with Almonds

🌲 MAKES 40 PIECES
🌲 PREPARATION TIME: 45 MINUTES +
🌲 COOKING TIME: 50 MINUTES

500 g (1 lb 2 oz) kataifi pastry
250 g (9 oz) unsalted butter, melted
125 g (4½ oz) ground pistachio nuts
200 g (7 oz) ground almonds
575 g (1 lb 4½ oz/2½ cups) caster
    (superfine) sugar
1 teaspoon ground cinnamon
¼ teaspoon ground cloves
1 tablespoon brandy
1 egg white
1 teaspoon lemon juice
5 cm (2 inch) piece lemon zest
4 whole cloves
1 cinnamon stick
1 tablespoon honey

Allow the kataifi pastry to come to room temperature, still in its packaging. This will take about 2 hours and makes the pastry easier to work with.

Preheat the oven to 170°C (325°F/Gas 3). Brush a 20 x 30 cm (8 x 12 inch) ovenproof dish or tray with some melted butter.

Put the nuts in a bowl with 115 g (4 oz/½ cup) of the caster sugar, the ground cinnamon, ground cloves and brandy. Lightly beat the egg white and add to the mixture. Stir to make a paste. Divide the mixture into eight portions and form each into a sausage shape about 18 cm (7 inches) long.

Take a small handful of the pastry strands and spread them out fairly compactly with the strands running lengthways towards you. The pastry should measure 18 x 25 cm (7 x 10 inches). Brush the pastry with melted butter. Place one of the 'nut' sausages along the end of the pastry nearest to you and roll up into a neat sausage shape. Repeat with the other pastry portions.

Place the rolls close together in the dish and brush them again with melted butter. Bake for 50 minutes, or until golden brown.

While the pastries are cooking, put the remaining sugar in a small saucepan with 500 ml (17 fl oz/2 cups) water and stir over low heat until dissolved. Add the lemon juice, lemon zest, whole cloves and cinnamon stick and boil together for 10 minutes. Stir in the honey, then set aside until cold.

When the pastries come out of the oven, pour the syrup over the top. Leave them to cool completely before cutting each roll into five pieces.

NOTES: It is very important that the syrup is cold and the kataifi hot when pouring the syrup over, otherwise the liquid will not be absorbed well or evenly.

Chocolate Strawberries

🔻 SERVES 8–10
🔻 PREPARATION TIME: 10 MINUTES +
🔻 COOKING TIME: 5 MINUTES

250 g (9 oz) strawberries
150 g (5½ oz) dark chocolate
100 g (3½ oz) white chocolate

Brush the strawberries with a dry pastry brush to remove any dirt. Melt the dark chocolate in a small heatproof bowl over a saucepan of steaming water, making sure the base of the bowl does not touch the water. Dip the bottom half of each strawberry in the chocolate. Put on a baking tray lined with baking paper and allow to set.

When set, melt the white chocolate in the same way as the dark. Dip the tips of the strawberries in the chocolate and allow to set on the baking tray.

Chocolate Meringue Kisses

🔻 MAKES 25
🔻 PREPARATION TIME: 20 MINUTES +
🔻 COOKING TIME: 40 MINUTES

2 egg whites, at room temperature
115 g (4 oz/½ cup) caster (superfine) sugar
¼ teaspoon ground cinnamon

FILLING
125 g (4½ oz) dark chocolate melts (buttons)
90 g (3¼ oz/⅓ cup) sour cream

Preheat the oven to 150°C (300°F/Gas 2). Line two baking trays with baking paper. Beat the egg whites using electric beaters in a small, clean, dry bowl until soft peaks form. Add the sugar gradually, beating thoroughly after each addition until stiffened and glossy peaks form. Add the cinnamon and beat until just combined. Transfer the mixture to a piping (icing) bag fitted with a 1 cm (½ inch) fluted nozzle. Pipe small stars of 1.5 cm (⅝ inch) diameter onto the trays, 3 cm (1¼ inches) apart. Bake for 30 minutes, or until pale and crisp. Turn off the oven. Leave the meringues to cool in the oven with the door ajar.

To make the filling, place the chocolate and sour cream in a small heatproof bowl. Bring a saucepan of water to the boil, remove from the heat and sit the bowl over the pan, making sure the base of the bowl does not touch the water. Stir occasionally until the chocolate has melted. Remove from the heat and cool slightly. Sandwich the meringues together with the chocolate filling.

Chocolate Strawberries

Pine Nut Tarts

⋏ MAKES 24
⋏ PREPARATION TIME: 25 MINUTES
⋏ COOKING TIME: 20 MINUTES

60 g (2¼ oz/½ cup) plain (all-purpose)
   flour
60 g (2¼ oz) unsalted butter, chopped
40 g (1½ oz/¼ cup) pine nuts
20 g (¾ oz) unsalted butter, extra, melted
175 g (6 oz/½ cup) golden syrup or dark
   corn syrup
2 tablespoons soft brown sugar
icing (confectioners') sugar, to dust
   (optional)

Preheat the oven to 180°C (350°F/Gas 4). Grease two 12-hole mini muffin tins. Sift the flour into a bowl. Using your fingertips, rub in the butter until the mixture resembles fine breadcrumbs. Turn onto a lightly floured surface and gather together.

Roll out on a lightly floured work surface to a thickness of 3 mm (⅛ inch). Cut out rounds with a 5 cm (2 inch) fluted cutter. Lift gently with a flat-bladed knife and line each muffin hole with pastry. Spread the pine nuts onto a flat baking tray and bake for 2–3 minutes, or until just golden. Remove from the tray and cool. Divide the nuts among the pastry cases.

Combine the melted butter, golden syrup and sugar and whisk with a fork, then pour over the pine nuts. Bake for 15 minutes, or until golden. Cool in the tins for 5 minutes before lifting out onto a wire rack to cool completely. Dust with icing sugar before serving, if desired.

Petits Fours

🔺 MAKES 32
🔺 PREPARATION TIME: 45 MINUTES
🔺 COOKING TIME: 20 MINUTES

2 eggs
55 g (2 oz/¼ cup) caster (superfine)
    sugar
85 g (3 oz/⅔ cup) plain (all-purpose)
    flour
30 g (1 oz) unsalted butter, melted

TOPPING
315 g (11 oz/1 cup) apricot jam, warmed
    and strained
2 teaspoons liqueur
200 g (7 oz) marzipan
400 g (14 oz) ready-made soft icing,
    chopped
small coloured fondant flowers,
    to decorate (optional)

Preheat the oven to 180°C (350°F/Gas 4). Lightly grease two 4.5 x 8 x 26 cm (1¾ x 3 x 10½ inch) loaf (bar) tins. Line the bases and sides with baking paper.

Beat the eggs and sugar in a bowl using electric beaters for 5 minutes, until very thick and pale. Fold in the sifted flour and melted butter quickly and lightly, using a metal spoon. Divide between the tins and bake for 15 minutes, or until lightly golden and springy to the touch. Leave in the tins for 3 minutes before turning out onto a wire rack to cool.

Using a 3 cm (1¼ inch) round cutter, cut out small rounds from the cakes. Brush the top and sides of each with the combined jam and liqueur. Roll the marzipan out to a thickness of 2 mm (⅛ inch) and cut out rounds and strips to cover the top and sides of the cakes.

Put the icing and 2 tablespoons water in a heatproof bowl and stand the bowl over a saucepan of simmering water. Stir until the icing has melted and the mixture is smooth. Allow to cool slightly.

Put the marzipan-covered cakes on a wire rack over a tray. Spoon the icing over each cake and use a flat-bladed knife to spread evenly over the base and sides. Reheat the icing over the saucepan if it begins to thicken. Leave the cakes to set. Carefully lift from the rack and put each in a paper petit four case. Decorate with small coloured fondant flowers, if desired.

NOTE: Petits fours will keep for up to 2 days in an airtight container in a cool, dark place. Store in a single layer.

Brandy Snaps

🔺 MAKES 15

🔺 PREPARATION TIME: 30 MINUTES

🔺 COOKING TIME: 15 MINUTES

60 g (2¼ oz) unsalted butter

2 tablespoons golden syrup or dark corn syrup

60 g (2¼ oz/⅓ cup) soft brown sugar

30 g (1 oz/¼ cup) plain (all-purpose) flour

1½ teaspoons ground ginger

60 g (2¼ oz) dark chocolate, chopped

Preheat the oven to 180°C (350°F/Gas 4). Line two baking trays with baking paper. Place the butter, golden syrup and sugar in a small saucepan and stir over low heat until the butter has melted and the sugar has dissolved. Remove from the heat and add the sifted flour and ground ginger to the saucepan. Use a wooden spoon to stir the mixture until the ingredients are well combined, taking care not to overbeat.

For each brandy snap, drop 3 level teaspoons of the mixture onto the trays about 12 cm (4½ inches) apart. Bake for 5–6 minutes, or until lightly browned. Leave the biscuits (cookies) on the trays for 30 seconds then, while still hot, lift one biscuit off the tray, using a large flat knife or spatula, and wrap around the handle of a thin wooden spoon. Slide the biscuit off the spoon and set aside to cool while you curl the remaining brandy snaps.

Put the chopped chocolate in a heatproof bowl. Bring a saucepan of water to the boil, remove from the heat and place the bowl over the water, making sure the base of the bowl does not touch the water. Stir occasionally until the chocolate has melted.

Dip both ends of each brandy snap in the melted chocolate and leave to dry on a foil-lined tray.

NOTE: There is a real art to making these biscuits: work quickly, as they harden and crack when cooled. If they cool too much, return them to the oven for a few minutes to warm, then try again.

White Cake Truffles

🔺 MAKES ABOUT 25
🔺 PREPARATION TIME: 25 MINUTES
🔺 COOKING TIME: 5 MINUTES

250 g (9 oz) Madeira (pound) cake crumbs
2 tablespoons chopped glacé orange peel
    or glacé apricots
1 tablespoon apricot jam
2 tablespoons cream
100 g (3½ oz) white chocolate, melted
gold leaf, to decorate (optional)

CHOCOLATE COATING
150 g (5½ oz) white chocolate, chopped
20 g (¾ oz) Copha (white vegetable
    shortening), chopped

Line a baking tray with foil. Combine the cake crumbs in a bowl with the chopped peel or apricots, jam, cream and melted chocolate. Mix until smooth, then roll into balls using 2 teaspoons of mixture for each ball.

To make the chocolate coating, combine the chocolate and shortening in a heatproof bowl. Bring a saucepan of water to the boil, remove from the heat and sit the bowl over the pan, making sure the base of the bowl does not touch the water. Stir occasionally until the chocolate and shortening have melted. Dip the balls in the chocolate, wipe the excess off on the edge of the bowl and leave them to set on the tray. Decorate with gold leaf, if desired.

NOTE: These truffles can be made up to 2 weeks ahead.

Rich Chocolate Truffles

🔺 MAKES ABOUT 30
🔺 PREPARATION TIME: 40 MINUTES +
🔺 COOKING TIME: 5 MINUTES

185 ml (6 fl oz/¾ cup) thick
    (double/heavy) cream
400 g (14 oz) dark chocolate, grated
70 g (2½ oz) unsalted butter, chopped
2 tablespoons Cointreau
dark unsweetened cocoa powder,
    for rolling

Put the cream in a small saucepan and bring to the boil. Remove from the heat and stir in the chocolate until it is completely melted. Add the butter and stir until melted. Stir in the Cointreau. Transfer to a large bowl, cover and refrigerate for several hours or overnight, or until firm enough to roll.

Quickly roll tablespoons of the mixture into balls, and refrigerate until firm. Roll the balls in the cocoa, shake off any excess and return to the refrigerator. Serve at room temperature.

NOTE: The truffle mixture can be made and rolled up to 2 weeks ahead. You will need to roll the balls in cocoa again close to serving time.

White Cake Truffles

Mini Toffee Apples

⚶ MAKES 6–8
⚶ PREPARATION TIME: 10 MINUTES
⚶ COOKING TIME: 10 MINUTES

2 large apples
200 g (7 oz) sugar

Peel the apples and use a melon baller to cut out balls, or cut the apples into cubes. Push a cocktail stick into each ball or cube.

Sprinkle the sugar in an even layer over the base of a saucepan and melt over low heat, slowly tipping the pan from side to side to make sure the sugar melts evenly. Keep the sugar moving so it does not start to colour on one side before the other side has melted. When the caramel starts to colour, keep swirling until you have an even colour, then remove the pan from the heat and stop the cooking by plunging the base into cold water. Reheat the caramel gently until runny.

Dip each piece of apple in the caramel, coating completely. Leave to dry, standing upright on a piece of baking paper. Reheat the caramel when necessary.

Florentines

⚶ MAKES 12
⚶ PREPARATION TIME: 25 MINUTES +
⚶ COOKING TIME: 15 MINUTES

55 g (2 oz) unsalted butter
45 g (1¾ oz/¼ cup) soft brown sugar
2 teaspoons honey
25 g (1 oz/¼ cup) flaked almonds, roughly chopped
2 tablespoons chopped dried apricots
2 tablespoons chopped glacé cherries
2 tablespoons mixed peel (mixed candied citrus peel)
40 g (1½ oz/⅓ cup) plain (all-purpose) flour, sifted
120 g (4¼ oz) dark chocolate, broken into small pieces

Preheat the oven to 180°C (350°F/Gas 4). Line two large baking trays with baking paper. Place the butter, sugar and honey in a saucepan and stir over low heat until the butter is melted and all the ingredients are combined. Remove from the heat and add the almonds, apricots, glacé cherries, mixed peel and flour. Mix well.

Place level tablespoons of the mixture well apart on the trays. Flatten the biscuits into 5 cm (2 inch) rounds, gently reshaping any before cooking. Bake for 10 minutes, or until lightly browned. Cool slightly on the tray before transferring onto a wire rack.

Put the dark chocolate in a heatproof bowl. Bring a small saucepan of water to the boil, remove from the heat and place the bowl over the pan, making sure the base of the bowl does not touch the water. Stir until melted. Spread on the base of each florentine and, using a fork, make a wavy pattern on the chocolate before it sets. Let the chocolate set before serving.

Mini Toffee Apples

Turkish Delight

🔺 MAKES 25 PIECES
🔺 PREPARATION TIME: 10 MINUTES
🔺 COOKING TIME: 1 HOUR

880 g (1 lb 15 oz/4 cups) sugar
125 g (4$\frac{1}{2}$ oz/1 cup) cornflour
    (cornstarch)
1 teaspoon cream of tartar
2 tablespoons rosewater
red food colouring
40 g (1$\frac{1}{2}$ oz/$\frac{1}{3}$ cup) icing
    (confectioners') sugar

Pour 625 ml (21$\frac{1}{2}$ fl oz/2$\frac{1}{2}$ cups) water into a large heavy-based saucepan and bring to the boil. Add the sugar and stir until thoroughly dissolved. Remove from the heat.

In a bowl, blend the cornflour and cream of tartar with 250 ml (9 fl oz/1 cup) cold water. Gradually add the blended cornflour to the sugar syrup, then return the saucepan to medium heat and stir until the mixture boils.

Reduce the heat and cook very slowly for 45 minutes, stirring frequently. During this time, the colour will change from cloudy to clear and golden, and the mixture will thicken.

Add the rosewater and a few drops of food colouring. Pour onto a lightly oiled 20 x 30 cm (8 x 12 inch) baking tray and leave to set. When firm and cool, cut into 2 cm ($\frac{3}{4}$ inch) squares and toss in the icing sugar.

Biscotti

🔺 MAKES 45
🔺 PREPARATION TIME: 25 MINUTES
🔺 COOKING TIME: 50 MINUTES

250 g (9 oz/2 cups) plain (all-purpose) flour
1 teaspoon baking powder
230 g (8 oz/1 cup) caster (superfine) sugar
3 eggs
1 egg yolk
1 teaspoon natural vanilla extract
1 teaspoon grated orange zest
110 g (3¾ oz/¾ cup) pistachio nuts

Preheat the oven to 180°C (350°F/Gas 4). Line two baking trays with baking paper and lightly dust with flour.

Sift the flour and baking powder into a large bowl. Add the sugar and mix well. Make a well in the centre and add two whole eggs, the egg yolk, vanilla extract and orange zest. Using a large metal spoon, stir until just combined. Mix in the pistachios. Knead for 2–3 minutes on a floured surface. The dough will be stiff at first. Sprinkle a little water onto the dough. Divide the mixture into two portions and roll each into a log about 25 cm (10 inches) long and 8 cm (3¼ inches) wide. Slightly flatten the tops.

Place the logs on the trays, allowing room for spreading. Beat the remaining egg and brush over the logs to glaze. Bake for 35 minutes, then remove from the oven.

Reduce the oven to 150°C (300°F/Gas 2). Allow the logs to cool slightly and cut each into 1 cm (½ inch) slices. Place, flat side down, on the trays and bake for 8 minutes. Turn the biscuits over and cook for a further 8 minutes, or until slightly coloured and crisp and dry. Transfer to a wire rack to cool completely. Store in an airtight container.

Madeleines

🔺 MAKES 12
🔺 PREPARATION TIME: 20 MINUTES
🔺 COOKING TIME: 15 MINUTES

125 g (4½ oz/1 cup) plain (all-purpose)
    flour
2 eggs
170 g (6 oz/¾ cup) caster (superfine)
    sugar
185 g (6½ oz) unsalted butter, melted
    and cooled
1 teaspoon finely grated orange zest
2 tablespoons icing (confectioners') sugar,
    to dust

Preheat the oven to 180°C (350°F/Gas 4). Lightly grease a 12-hole madeleine tin or shallow patty pan. Lightly dust the madeleine tin with flour and shake off any excess.

Sift the flour three times onto baking paper. Combine the eggs and sugar in a heatproof bowl. Place the bowl over a saucepan of simmering water, making sure the base of the bowl does not touch the water, and beat the mixture using a whisk or electric beaters until thick and pale yellow. Remove the bowl from the heat and continue to beat the mixture until cooled slightly and increased in volume.

Add the sifted flour, butter and orange zest to the bowl and fold in quickly and lightly with a metal spoon until just combined. Spoon the mixture carefully into the madeleine holes. Bake for 10–12 minutes, or until lightly golden. Carefully remove from the tin and transfer to a wire rack to cool. Dust with icing sugar before serving. Madeleines are best eaten on the day of baking.

Little Lemon Tarts

⚶ MAKES 24
⚶ PREPARATION TIME: 40 MINUTES +
⚶ COOKING TIME: 15 MINUTES

250 g (9 oz/2 cups) plain (all-purpose)
    flour
125 g (4 1/2 oz) unsalted butter, chopped
2 teaspoons caster (superfine) sugar
1 teaspoon grated lemon zest
1 egg yolk

FILLING
125 g (4 1/2 oz) cream cheese, softened
115 g (4 oz/1/2 cup) caster (superfine)
    sugar
2 egg yolks
2 tablespoons lemon juice
160 g (5 3/4 oz/1/2 cup) sweetened
    condensed milk
strips of candied lemon peel, to garnish
    (optional)

Preheat the oven to 180°C (350°F/Gas 4). Brush two round-based 12-cup shallow patty pans or mini muffin tins with oil. Sift the flour and a pinch of salt into a bowl and rub in the butter until it resembles fine breadcrumbs. Add the sugar, zest, egg yolk and 2–3 tablespoons of iced water and, with a flat-bladed knife, use a cutting action until a rough dough forms. Gently knead on a lightly floured surface until smooth. Cover in plastic wrap and chill for 10 minutes.

To make the filling, beat the cream cheese, sugar and egg yolks using electric beaters until smooth and thickened. Add the lemon juice and condensed milk and beat until well combined.

Roll out the dough between sheets of baking paper to a round 3 mm (about 1/8 inch) thick. Using a 7 cm (2 3/4 inch) fluted round cutter, cut rounds from the pastry. Gently press into the patty tins. Lightly prick each round three times. Bake for 10 minutes, or until just starting to turn golden. Remove from the oven and spoon 2 teaspoons of filling into each case. Return to the oven for a further 5 minutes, or until the filling has set. Cool slightly before removing from the tins. Garnish with strips of candied lemon peel, if desired.

Baklava Fingers

🔺 MAKES 24
🔺 PREPARATION TIME: 30 MINUTES
🔺 COOKING TIME: 25 MINUTES

FILLING
90 g (3¼ oz/¾ cup) walnut pieces,
    finely chopped
1 tablespoon soft brown sugar
1 teaspoon ground cinnamon
20 g (¾ oz) unsalted butter, melted

8 sheets filo pastry
50 g (1¾ oz) unsalted butter, melted

SYRUP
220 g (7¾ oz/1 cup) sugar
2 tablespoons honey
2 teaspoons orange flower water (optional)

Preheat the oven to 210°C (415°F/Gas 6–7). Brush a baking tray with oil or melted butter.

To make the filling, put the walnuts, sugar, cinnamon and butter in a small bowl and stir until combined.

Remove one sheet of filo and cover the rest with a damp tea towel (dish towel) to prevent them from drying out. Place the sheet of filo pastry on a work bench, brush with melted butter and fold in half. Cut the sheet into three strips and place a heaped teaspoon of filling close to the front edge of the pastry. Roll up, tucking in the edges. Place on the prepared tray and brush with melted butter.

Repeat with the remaining pastry sheets. Bake for 15 minutes, or until golden brown.

To make the syrup, combine the sugar, honey and 125 ml (4 fl oz/½ cup) water in a small saucepan. Stir over low heat, without boiling, until the sugar has completely dissolved. Bring to the boil, reduce the heat and simmer for 5 minutes. Remove from the heat and add the orange flower water.

Transfer the pastries to a wire rack set over a tray and spoon the syrup over the pastries while both the pastries and syrup are still warm.

NOTE: Store in an airtight container for up to 2 days.

Nougat

⟁ MAKES 1 KG (2 LB 4 OZ)
⟁ PREPARATION TIME: 30 MINUTES +
⟁ COOKING TIME: 15 MINUTES

440 g (15½ oz/2 cups) sugar
250 ml (9 fl oz/1 cup) liquid glucose
175 g (6 oz/½ cup) honey
2 egg whites
1 teaspoon natural vanilla extract
125 g (4½ oz) unsalted butter, softened
60 g (2¼ oz) almonds, unblanched
   and toasted
100 g (3½ oz) glacé (candied) cherries

Grease a 18 x 28 cm (7 x 11 inch) baking dish and line with baking paper. Put the sugar, glucose, honey, 60 ml (2 fl oz/¼ cup) water and ¼ teaspoon salt in a heavy-based saucepan and stir over low heat until dissolved. Bring to the boil and cook at a rolling boil for 8 minutes, or until the mixture reaches 122°C (225°F) on a sugar thermometer. The correct temperature is very important, otherwise the mixture will not set properly.

Beat the egg whites in a clean, dry bowl with electric beaters until stiff peaks form. Slowly pour one-quarter of the sugar mixture onto the egg whites in a thin stream and beat for up to 5 minutes, or until the mixture holds its shape. Put the remaining syrup over the heat and cook for 2 minutes (watch that it doesn't burn), or until a small amount forms brittle threads when dropped in cold water, or reaches 157°C (315°F) on a sugar thermometer. Pour slowly onto the meringue mixture with the beaters running and beat until the mixture is very thick.

Add the vanilla and butter and beat for a further 5 minutes. Stir in the almonds and cherries with a metal spoon. Turn the mixture into the tin and smooth the top with a palette knife. Refrigerate for at least 4 hours, or until firm. Turn out onto a large chopping board. Cut into 2 x 4 cm (³/4 x 1½ inch) pieces. Wrap each piece in cellophane and store in the refrigerator.

Coconut Macaroons

🔺 MAKES 60
🔺 PREPARATION TIME: 25 MINUTES
🔺 COOKING TIME: 40 MINUTES

3 egg whites
310 g (11 oz) caster (superfine) sugar
1 teaspoon grated lemon zest
½ teaspoon natural coconut extract
2 tablespoons cornflour (cornstarch), sifted
270 g (9¾ oz/3 cups) desiccated coconut

Preheat the oven to 160°C (315°F/Gas 2–3). Line two baking trays with baking paper.

Beat the egg whites in a clean, dry bowl using electric beaters until soft peaks form. Gradually add the sugar, beating constantly until thick and glossy and the sugar has dissolved. Add the lemon zest and coconut extract and beat until just combined. Add the cornflour and desiccated coconut and stir gently with a metal spoon.

Drop heaped teaspoons onto the trays, about 3 cm (1¼ inches) apart – you will need to do this in batches. Bake for 15–20 minutes, or until golden. Remove from the tins and cool. Repeat to use all the macaroon mixture. Allow to cool.

Chocolate Tarts

🔺 MAKES ABOUT 45
🔺 PREPARATION TIME: 40 MINUTES +
🔺 COOKING TIME: 30 MINUTES

PASTRY
155 g (5½ oz/1¼ cups) plain
    (all-purpose) flour
75 g (2¾ oz) unsalted butter, chopped
55 g (2 oz/¼ cup) caster (superfine)
    sugar
2 egg yolks

250 g (9 oz) dark chocolate, finely
    chopped
250 ml (9 fl oz/1 cup) cream
1 tablespoon orange-flavoured liqueur
1 orange
115 g (4 oz/½ cup) caster (superfine)
    sugar, extra
unsweetened cocoa powder, to dust

Lightly grease two 12-hole tartlet tins. To make the pastry, sift the flour into a large bowl and add the butter. Rub in with your fingertips until the mixture resembles fine breadcrumbs. Stir in the sugar. Make a well in the centre and add the egg yolks and up to 2 tablespoons water. Mix with a flat-bladed knife using a cutting action, until the mixture comes together in beads. Gather together and lift out onto a lightly floured work surface. Press into a ball and flatten slightly into a disc. Wrap in plastic wrap and refrigerate for 20 minutes.

Preheat the oven to 180°C (350°F/Gas 4). Roll the dough between two sheets of baking paper and cut rounds with a 5 cm (2 inch) cutter. Press into the tins.

Bake for about 10 minutes, or until lightly browned. Remove from the tins and cool. Repeat to use all the pastry. Allow to cool.

Put the chocolate in a heatproof bowl. Bring the cream to the boil in a small saucepan and pour over the chocolate. Leave for 1 minute, then stir until the chocolate has melted. Stir in the liqueur. Allow to set, stirring occasionally until thick.

Meanwhile, thinly peel the orange, avoiding the bitter white pith, and cut the peel into short thin strips. Put the extra sugar, peel and 125 ml (4 fl oz/½ cup) of water in a small saucepan, stir over heat until the sugar has dissolved, then simmer for about 5–10 minutes, or until thick and syrupy. Remove the peel with tongs, drain on baking paper and allow to cool.

Spoon the chocolate mixture into a piping (icing) bag fitted with a 1 cm (½ inch) plain piping nozzle. Pipe three small blobs of mixture into the pastry case, pulling up as you pipe so the mixture forms a point. Dust with cocoa, decorate with the orange zest and refrigerate until ready to serve.